praise for

food: the good girl's drug

"Sunny Sea Gold is one of the best and most compassionate educators about women's health issues out there. She is especially strong on the emotional underpinnings of health conditions such as eating disorders and obsessive thinking about body image that have deep roots in a gender context. Anyone who is concerned about the emotional roots of her (or his) food or body issues will be enlightened and helped by Gold's clear, well-informed, evocative, and caring exploration."

—Naomi Wolf, author of the *New York Times* bestsellers *The Beauty Myth, The End of America* and *Give Me Liberty*

"Sunny Gold has found the formula for using her own experience of recovering from binge eating disorder to motivate others to triumph over theirs. This is not a passive read! Sunny engages us with her own stories and those of other good girls who have used food as a drug, and then creates a 3-D reading experience with exercises, thought questions, and advice on how to develop a toolkit to overcome an unhealthy relationship with food. Reading *Food: The Good Girl's Drug* feels less like reading a book and more like participating in a motivational workshop."

—Cynthia M. Bulik, Ph.D., director, University of North Carolina Eating Disorders Program and author of *Crave: Why You Binge Eat and How to Stop*

"Sharing deeply personal stories of hope and recovery from the prison of problematic relationships with food, eating, and exercise, Sunny Gold and the brave women who with her offer their insights contribute to a comprehensive survey of the topic in a manner that is remarkably, if you will. . . . easily digestible."

—Dr. Drew Pinsky, M.D., host of *Celebrity Rehab with Dr. Drew*

"Sunny Sea Gold has created more than a recovery bible for binge eaters—she's shined a light on a wickedly dark chapter in many women's lives, where food and secret eating become substitutes for love, and authentic connection. The insights and exercises in this book are relative, easy to do, and can be really quite a valuable tool in moving beyond overeating and creating a life where food is nutrition and self-love is abundant."

—Jessica Weiner, self-esteem expert and author of
Life Doesn't Begin 5 Pounds from Now

"As I travel the country talking to young women about self esteem, I find that *far* too many are obsessed with dieting and being thin. Their obsessions often backfire into overeating and feeling out of control about food, so I'm happy I now have a book to recommend to them that will help them get normal about food and their bodies again."

—Whitney Thompson, winner of America's Next Top Model, Cycle 10,
founder of ShopSupermodel.com

"A wonderfully honest, insightful, and important resource for understanding the challenges, pain, and confusion of binge eating disorder. Sunny Sea Gold has masterfully woven her own personal experiences throughout, sharing assurances that those affected by the illness are not alone but recovery is achievable, and the hope for a normal healthy life is possible. This is a timely must read for the weight-focused world, to grasp that not all eating disorders look alike, but they do all create personal hardship and health risks."

—Lynn S. Grefe, president and CEO, National Eating Disorders Association

"*Food: The Good Girl's* Drug is a must read for anyone, anywhere along their path to recovery from binge eating. Filled with actionable tools, rich insight, and expert knowledge, this book helps the reader develop a practical skill set to live their life beyond eating disorders. Truly a compelling, authentic, and invaluable book!"

—Johanna Kandel, executive director of The Alliance for
Eating Disorders and author of *Life Beyond Your Eating Disorder*

food: the good girl's drug

How to Stop Using Food to Control Your Feelings

SUNNY SEA GOLD

B

BERKLEY BOOKS, NEW YORK

THE BERKLEY PUBLISHING GROUP
Published by the Penguin Group
Penguin Group (USA) Inc.
375 Hudson Street, New York, New York 10014, USA
Penguin Group (Canada), 90 Eglinton Avenue East, Suite 700, Toronto, Ontario M4P 2Y3, Canada
(a division of Pearson Penguin Canada Inc.)
Penguin Books Ltd., 80 Strand, London WC2R 0RL, England
Penguin Group Ireland, 25 St. Stephen's Green, Dublin 2, Ireland (a division of Penguin Books Ltd.)
Penguin Group (Australia), 250 Camberwell Road, Camberwell, Victoria 3124, Australia
(a division of Pearson Australia Group Pty. Ltd.)
Penguin Books India Pvt. Ltd., 11 Community Centre, Panchsheel Park, New Delhi—110 017, India
Penguin Group (NZ), 67 Apollo Drive, Rosedale, North Shore, 0632, New Zealand
(a division of Pearson New Zealand Ltd.)
Penguin Books (South Africa) (Pty.) Ltd., 24 Sturdee Avenue, Rosebank, Johannesburg 2196,
South Africa

Penguin Books Ltd., Registered Offices: 80 Strand, London WC2R 0RL, England

Every effort has been made to ensure that the information contained in this book is complete and accurate. However, neither the publisher nor the author is engaged in rendering professional advice or services to the individual reader. The ideas, procedures, and suggestions contained in this book are not intended as a substitute for consulting with your physician. All matters regarding your health require medical supervision. Neither the author nor the publisher shall be liable or responsible for any loss or damage allegedly arising from any information or suggestion in this book.

While the author has made every effort to provide accurate telephone numbers and Internet addresses at the time of publication, neither the publisher nor the author assumes any responsibility for errors, or for changes that occur after publication. Further, publisher does not have any control over and does not assume any responsibility for author or third-party websites or their content.

PRINTING HISTORY
Berkley trade paperback edition / April 2011

Library of Congress Cataloging-in-Publication Data

Gold, Sunny Sea.
    Food : the good girl's drug : how to stop using food to control your feelings / Sunny Sea Gold.
        p.   cm.
    Includes bibliographical references.
        ISBN 978-0-425-23903-2 (pbk.)
    1. Compulsive eating—Psychological aspects.   2. Food—Psychological aspects.   3. Eating disorders—Patients—Rehabilitation.   I. Title.
        RC552.C65G65   2011
        616.85'2606—dc22   2010050177

PRINTED IN THE UNITED STATES OF AMERICA

10 9 8 7 6 5 4 3 2 1

This book is dedicated to every young woman
who has ever hated her body and felt out-of-control
about food, including the twenty-four brave and incredibly
honest young women who shared their stories of struggle and
recovery for this book. Keep moving forward and
you can live a life that's healthy, happy, and free!

contents

part three: living your life without relying on the good girl's drug

acknowledgments

My mother, Melinda Schnarre, and my father, Richard Green, are two very brave souls. While writing this book, I sent them each chapter as I finished it, always worried that one or both would call or e-mail to say they were hurt by something and they wanted me to make a change. That never happened. My parents were both incredibly supportive—100 percent willing to allow me to put their divorce, our family's home life, and even their personal quirks on display in order to help girls and women who are suffering with food the way I once did. I respect them immensely for that, and am grateful. My stepfather, George, was equally supportive, and I thank him for that—and all the late-night talks we had when I was a teenager, too.

Of course, no one was more helpful to me throughout the process of writing this book than my husband, John. For six months during the winter and spring of 2010—during our very first year of marriage—I dedicated nearly all of my free time, and every single weekend, to interviewing girls and experts, researching, and writing. John never complained, even when he had to do all the laundry and grocery shopping. He's the best partner a girl could ask for.

There's an amazing group of women to whom I will be eternally grateful and without whom this book would not have been possible: the women of the Woodhull Institute for Ethical Leadership, a nonprofit organization that provides leadership training and professional development for women. First, I owe Kristen Kemp, herself the author of some fourteen books and a lecturer for Woodhull, a thank-you. She's the one who first told Wende Jager-Hyman, Woodhull's executive director, about the book I wanted to write. Kristen knew that once the cat was out of the bag, Wende wouldn't let me chicken out or drop the ball. And Wendy didn't. She immediately signed me up for a nonfiction writer's retreat during which Woodhull cofounder and famous feminist author Naomi Wolf taught me and several other starstruck students how to create and write a book proposal. After leaving that workshop—and getting a thumbs-up on the idea from Naomi—I knew this book was important and I would do whatever it took to get it published. Wende's involvement didn't end there. She also introduced me to her nonfiction author daughter, Joie, who, in turn, introduced me to her literary agent, Laurie Abkemeier.

When I met Laurie, I knew I had found the smart, savvy, and dedicated partner I needed to sell this book—which she did in just six weeks! Laurie is a former book editor herself, and was just the right mix of creative and no-nonsense businesswoman for a nervous first-time author like me. I'm grateful for all of her input, from the proposal stage to the cover, to the finished manuscript.

Thank you also to Morgan Holland, the research assistant who helped me keep HealthyGirl.org afloat with her incredibly astute and insightful blog posts while I was typing furiously away on my laptop.

An enormous thank-you to my colleagues and mentors in the magazine world, namely Wendy Naugle, Jill Herzig, and Marlene Kahan. With your support, my years in this dream career have also been key to making the dream of writing this book a reality. The lessons I've learned about women's health, about writing, and about acknowledgments

myself while working at *Glamour* and *Redbook* have been absolutely invaluable.

And finally, a heartfelt thank-you to my editor, Denise Silvestro, to her assistant, Meredith Giordan, and everyone at Berkley Books. Thank you for believing in this project as much as I do.

foreword

During my eleven years working with women at the Renfrew Center's nationally renowned eating disorders treatment facilities, I've seen too many young women struggle with dieting, starving, and bingeing in secret, thinking they just have a willpower problem and aren't "sick enough" to get the help that they need. And even when they do reach out, the fact is, there aren't as many resources out there for people dealing with binge eating as there are for those with anorexia or bulimia. Research indicates that binge eating is more common than other eating disorders like anorexia or bulimia—yet it is talked about the least. That's one reason why I am so excited to be a part of this book.

Sometimes you meet someone even for a brief moment and

you know that they are here to do good on the planet. And you want to support them in their goodness and to be a part of that if even in a small way. That was my experience during my first conversation with Sunny.

I first "met" Sunny over the phone when she was looking for therapists to interview for this book. She was familiar with the Renfrew Center's reputation and wanted to talk to a clinician here—so the marketing department referred her to me. After hearing her story, I was immediately on board with this book and with her mission to help young women who, like herself at one time, struggle with binge eating. I was struck by her authenticity and courage in sharing her own story, her genuine desire to help others, and her positive perspective on life—that no matter how bad things get, there is always hope.

Even in our very first conversation she seemed like a light to me (and not just because of her name!), wanting to help girls out of the dark places they were in as a result of their eating disorder. Eating disorders and food obsession extinguish a person's passions and sense of who they are and what they are capable of doing in the world. But this book is about showing people that there is another way to live, both in their own bodies and in the world.

Sunny shares in a deeply personal way how her own binge eating disorder began in her early teens—a very common time for food and body issues to begin or worsen—and the steps she took over the next several years that led to triumph over disordered eating. She asked dozens of other women between the ages of sixteen and thirty to share their stories too, and they all openly and honestly describe their behaviors with food and the strategies they've used to get better. Their stories inspire and give hope that recovery from binge eating is possible.

This book is not meant *only* to comfort, inform, and inspire—Sunny has also partnered with top experts and researchers in the eating disorders field to make sure it also provides specific tools, exercises, and resources that will assist in the healing process.

Food: The Good Girl's Drug couldn't have come soon enough: The obsession with weight in this country seems to be making things worse, not better. Eating disorders of all kinds are on the rise, and those of us who treat them are seeing younger and younger people who despise their bodies and struggle with issues of food.

For young women who are stuck in an out-of-control cycle of bingeing and dieting, this book could be the beginning of a life free from body hate and food obsession.

Jennifer Nardozzi, Psy.D.
National Training Manager, The Renfrew Center

part one:

understanding what's going on between you and food

chapter one

Would Someone Please Explain Why I Can't Stop Eating?

I love to eat—always have, always will. As a kid, I was a VIP member of the Clean Plate Club. You didn't have to tell me to finish my spaghetti, my sandwich, or even my veggies. I'd chow down every last bit of whatever was put in front of me and usually ask for more. And you know what? There was nothing wrong with that. I was, as my parents used to say, "a good little eater" and a healthy little girl.

But in my early teens, eating went from something fun, yummy, and nourishing to something that made me absolutely miserable. My parents had started fighting a lot, and ultimately talking divorce. I was freaking out. My family had always been really solid—no matter what I was going through, I could count on the fact that I had a mother and father who loved and supported me. My mom didn't even work outside of the home, so I had someone there every day after school. Honestly, it was pretty idyllic: I remember a couple of friends asking me if my mom was kidding around when she sweetly offered them a slice of homemade pineapple cake. Uh, nope. That was my life. Until it wasn't.

In addition to all of the other stuff I was going through as a fourteen- or fifteen-year-old—getting my braces off, feeling awkward, being backstabbed by friends, falling in love for the first time—my parents split up, my dad moved to another town, my mom started working two jobs and started dating (ouch). That's when a really puzzling, frenzied pattern of eating started to emerge. I snuck food, stole food, hid food, obsessed about food, loved food, hated food, hated myself. I would shove more food into my belly than I would've thought was humanly possible.

What I call my first official binge happened in the ninth grade. Mom and Dad were yelling at each other one night, and I escaped outside and dragged a blanket with me, heading for the roof of our German shepherd's doghouse so I wouldn't have to listen to it. Before I scooted out the door, I grabbed a spoon and a can of frozen orange juice concentrate from the freezer. (I'd seen my dad eating it before, and it wasn't half bad, sort of like really sweet sorbet.) I perched on the roof of that doghouse and cried, scooping the syrupy stuff into my mouth until the can was almost empty. I was in so much pain—even now, the memory of it brings a lump into my throat and a buzzy feeling in the pit of my stomach. But the sweetness of the juice and the mechanical action of moving the spoon up to my mouth over and over again seemed to numb my feelings.

I learned how to binge that night. I didn't know that's what it was called, all I knew was that it distracted me from my fear, hurt, and anger at what was going on in my family. So the next time I was hurting, I binged again. My mom was at one of her jobs (or maybe on a date?) and I invited my boyfriend over . . . to break up with him. Things had felt off for a couple of weeks and I finally realized I just wasn't that into him anymore. But after he left, I was feeling sad, lonely, and guilty for hurting such a sweet (and cute) guy. So what do you think I did? I ordered two small pizzas and ate them—all by myself. Then I hid the cardboard evidence deep in the outdoor garbage can. I woke up the next morning with puffy eyes and heartburn, feeling guilty, fat, and disgusting.

As much as I hated what I was doing with food, I couldn't stop. Soon I was sneaking into the kitchen almost every night, praying my mom wouldn't hear the wooden floors creak as I tiptoed past her bedroom door. I'd stand at the counter and eat three, four, five pieces of bread with butter, or pour maple syrup into peanut butter and eat it straight out of the jar. If there were cookies, ice cream, or crackers, I'd down those; if we had chips, I'd microwave a huge plate of them with shredded cheddar cheese on top for makeshift nachos.

The face-stuffing didn't just happen at home: When I baby-sat my neighbors' kids or cleaned their houses for extra cash, I spent half the time rifling through their cupboards for Little Debbie snacks and potato chips. I rarely, if ever, ate anything at school, but I did have a close friend who became sort of a "binge buddy." We'd go up to this Mexican place in our town called Rosa Maria's that was famous for its huge burritos—we'd each get one and go back to her room to devour them. Then we'd watch movies or play video games until we felt human again.

My crazy-fast teenage metabolism kept me slim for a while, but I eventually started putting on pounds. I slowly grew out of my jeans, size by size, and I hated myself for it. Though nowhere near it (yet), I thought I was fat. And "fat" to me meant disgusting, ugly, and weak. I started wearing big, baggy sweaters or sweatshirts over leggings to hide what I thought was an unacceptably big body, and I wore my long hair down all of the time to cover even more of myself. One Sunday afternoon, sobbing, I threw a pair of too-tight pants across my bedroom and screamed that I refused to wear anything larger. My mom stepped in and said she'd help—and asked a pharmacist friend to get me some diet pills. So there I was at fifteen years old, five six and probably 125 pounds, taking the prescription diet drug Tenuate. I felt shaky, nervous, and dry-mouthed, and I remember hoping my new boyfriend wouldn't notice my bad breath or pill-induced paranoia. It's obvious to my mother now that providing diet pills to her teenage daughter wasn't a smart or healthy thing for her to do. But at the time, she believed she was helping. She had very little understanding of eating disorders at all, had never heard of "emotional overeating" or binge eating, and saw me in great pain about putting on weight. She also had her own very deep-seated beliefs about the importance of being thin, and those likely played into it too. I'll talk a little more about that in Chapter 3 when we discuss how our family members' body image and dieting issues can affect our own.

While the diet pills worked during the day, they didn't keep me from eating at night—or even sometimes during the afternoons when I was home alone. My junior year of high school, I was selling candy bars for a school fund-raiser. One day after school, I ate one. Then two. Then three. Then four. I couldn't stop. I ate half a dozen candy bars that afternoon, and then spent the evening trying to make myself throw them up until my eyes were red and I was drooling into the toilet. But it didn't work. I couldn't get rid of the food, and I couldn't stop eating. Over the course of the two-month fund-raiser I downed at least forty dollars' worth of candy. At fifty cents apiece, that was eighty bars. *Eighty* bars.

My life became a cycle of out-of-control bingeing, guilt, dieting, and total self-hate that lasted all the way through my midtwenties. I thought about food, weight, and my body constantly: What should I eat? What shouldn't I eat? When can I eat again? How can I sneak this food into my room without my roommate noticing? Why am I so fat and ugly? Why can't I just STOP EATING? I felt like I was going insane. I didn't know it at the time, but I had an eating disorder. It wasn't anorexia (obviously), it wasn't bulimia (since I didn't make myself throw up after I ate); it was binge eating disorder (BED). I had no idea there even was such a thing, or that anyone else in the entire world ate this way. I just thought I was a pig and a freak.

What Is Binge Eating Disorder, and Do I Have It?

The official definition of binge eating disorder (BED) is evolving, but the National Eating Disorders Association (nationaleatingdisorders.org) describes it as recurrent binge eating without the regular use of compensatory measures—such as vomiting, excessive exercise, or using laxatives—to counter the binges. Some symptoms include:

- Frequent episodes of eating large quantities of food in relatively short periods of time
- Feeling out of control over eating behavior
- Feeling ashamed or disgusted by the behavior
- Eating rapidly
- Eating in secret
- Eating until uncomfortably full

Researchers estimate that 2 to 5 percent of Americans have binge eating disorder. It's more common than anorexia and bulimia combined, but it's not talked about as much. ✳

Of course, not everyone who overeats has binge eating disorder. Experts now recognize that there's a disordered eating spectrum, and that many people who have weird relationships with food move around on that spectrum throughout their lives, sometimes undereating, sometimes overeating, sometimes throwing up or using laxatives or diet pills. There's even a diagnosis called "eating disorder not otherwise specified" (EDNOS) that includes people who have symptoms of a few or even all of the other disorders.

"Most of the clients I see don't only use one behavior," said Jennifer Nardozzi, Psy.D., national training manager of The Renfrew Center eating disorder treatment clinics. "Throughout their lives, they engage in lots of things: dieting, overexercising, taking diet pills, bingeing. I find that even when people are mostly emotional eaters or bingers, they also diet or restrict. They're often not eating for hours and hours and then the bingeing occurs."

Twenty-five-year-old Razieh told me that she went from one extreme to the other. "My story with eating disorders started when I was nineteen. I was anorexic and an overexerciser for about a year and a half. Then I think my body just gave out one day and I reached for a granola bar that, at the time, was not on my structured 'eating plan.' Well, let's just say that one granola bar turned into about two hours of bingeing in the kitchen. From then on, my life revolved around eating—bingeing alone—and working out to make up for it." Eighteen-year-old Kendra sunny sea gold

used to binge and purge like a bulimic, but stopped throwing up when she read about some of the scary possible health effects of eating disorders, like infertility. "I quit purging, but unfortunately the bingeing part was more difficult to kick," she said.

What Eating Disorders Can Do to Your Body

Bingeing can cause chronic heartburn, bloating, diarrhea, and constipation, and cause lasting damage to your intestinal tract and stomach. Becoming obese from bingeing can increase your risk of heart disease, high blood pressure, infertility, diabetes, heart attack, stroke, and certain cancers, including breast cancer.

Vomiting can cause irreversible yellowing and erosion of the teeth or tooth loss, harm the stomach and throat, and lead to severe dehydration, seizures, heart attack, and potentially deadly electrolyte imbalances.

Taking laxatives can cause severe dehydration and even cause some women's digestive systems to become so dependent on the drugs that they no longer work properly on their own.

Starving can disrupt metabolism so that the body no longer burns calories at a normal rate, and may cause the body to leach nutrients from its own muscle and bone. Becoming very underweight can lead to infertility, heart failure, and even death.

Diet pills can cause racing heart beat, anxiety, bad breath, mood swings, dehydration, fainting, and can dangerously interact with some prescription medications like antidepressants.

Of course, an eating-disordered person isn't necessarily doomed to any of these fates. The earlier she gets help and starts treating her body more gently, and nourishing it—rather than punishing it—with food, the fewer lasting effects she'll have. ✳

What Exactly Is a "Binge," Anyway?

Eating disorder professionals define a binge as eating a large amount of food in a short period of time, and experiencing a feeling of being out of control while doing it. In reality though, bingeing means different things to different people—and binges can change throughout your life as you start to recover from your eating issues, said clinical psychologist Cynthia Bulik, Ph.D., director of the University of North Carolina eating disorders program. "We researchers spend hours figuring out what qualifies as a binge—and frankly I am not convinced that it's a great way to spend our time. At some point it becomes splitting hairs," she said. "The key issue is if it causes distress to the individual and/or interferes with their life in any way. That could mean not going out with friends to eat, avoiding social situations in which there is food, choosing to stay at home with your binge foods over going to work. In fact, there is also something we call 'subjective' binges, where the amount of food isn't actually that large, but the person still feels out of control. Someone might eat one chocolate chip cookie and feel like she is completely out of control—she transgressed her boundary for what was okay and feels like she binged."

My senior year in college, I was editor in chief of the daily campus newspaper and would often work until after midnight at the offices without eating dinner. On the way home, I'd pull into the Jack in the Box drive-through and order what might not have been an absolutely *insane* amount of food, but was certainly more than a healthy young woman needed. The sourdough Jack cheeseburger alone would've been enough to feed my body's actual hunger; the large order of deep-fried jalapeño poppers with a side of ranch dressing and the slice of cheesecake I used to feed my emotional hunger. "When soothing anxiety, I reach for sugar and carbs," Razieh told me. "Anything that I have been staring at all week, convincing myself not to eat, is usually the first thing I grab. But often it's the large variety of foods that defines my binges now. The thought of eating two slices of pizza for lunch will be too overwhelming, so I try to just have a couple of snacks instead. But that's not satisfying, so it leads to seven or eight small snacks, like a handful of nuts, a chocolate bar, a piece of bread, a yogurt, some popcorn and a granola bar—ultimately resulting in more calories than the two slices of pizza. It's so mental!"

My bingeing was at its worst in my early twenties. I was divorced (yes, divorced! I had a very brief marriage from twenty-one to twenty-three), depressed, lonely, and scared, and I relied on food to soothe myself. Two of my favorite binge foods during that time of my life were peanut butter M&M's and miniature Reese's peanut butter cups. I'd buy a big one-pound "family size" bag of one of those, and then go home, shut myself up in my room safe from the prying eyes of my roommates, and just eat. I'd shove the candy in my mouth as fast as possible, chewing like a machine, until I felt sick. A few times I remember having to lie facedown on my bed with a pillow under my belly to

---

A binge is defined as eating a large amount of food in a short period of time, and experiencing a feeling of being out of control while doing it.

---

soothe the pain. Sometimes, after my stomach felt better, I'd start eating again.

No one could call that behavior anything but disordered. But often bingeing and emotional eating are more subtle than that. "My binges are the result of stress, usually with school, but sometimes with family, too," said Trish, a twenty-three-year-old law student. "Law school is tough, and I find myself in pressure overloads more often than not, which leads me to binge unconsciously. I say 'unconsciously' because I am so focused on my schoolwork and applying for internships and moot court teams that I don't realize how much I actually eat, or what I'm putting in my mouth. I order Chinese food or sushi or pizza and I sit at my kitchen table with three hundred pages of criminal law to read, and I just put food into my mouth without so much as looking at it until I'm full. Then, once I realize that I just ate a whole container of General Tso's, I have my postbinge guilt trip. All of my focus comes off of my work and onto my flaws. I think about how I have no self-control, how I'm obese, and I look down at my belly in disgust and let my thoughts abuse me."

How Many People Binge Eat?

There are literally millions of us out there who struggle with emotional overeating and bingeing. It's estimated that 3.5 percent of women and 2 percent of men in the United States have binge eating disorder. Recent research has shown that binge eating is more common than anorexia and bulimia combined, and that kids as young as six years old can have problems with it. But bingeing isn't talked about as much as anorexia and bulimia, and that means there aren't nearly enough resources for those who need help, said Dr. Nardozzi.

I've often wondered why the discussion of binge eating is so much more muted than other disorders. It could be because it's simply not as—for lack of a better word—"glamorous" as the diseases that make people skinny. Just think about it: Tabloid covers explode with exclamation points and praise when a pop star "gets her bikini body back" and some of our most celebrated young female celebs are so skinny they look a little sick. Writers and bloggers titter about how stars look anorexic, but then go on to talk about how fashionable and cool they are. "There's still a negative stigma attached to overeating," said Charles Sophy, F.A.C.N., a psychiatrist in Beverly Hills who treats many young women with disordered eating, including some in the entertainment industry. "This is especially true for women, where it is oftentimes viewed as being unfeminine. But being skinny, even too skinny, can be associated with determination or what someone may have to sacrifice in order to pursue a certain career path. Those superskinny people seem to have it all together, while being overweight can be associated with what people think of as a lack of discipline or laziness, and a general lack of

> There are literally millions of us out there who struggle with emotional overeating and bingeing. It's estimated that 3.5 percent of women and 2 percent of men in the United States have binge eating disorder.

control. Many times that's untrue, just like the idea that skinny people have it all together."

Still, the message we girls and women get is all too clear: Being skinny—even if you have to starve or throw up to get that way—is pretty and glamorous; eating too much and getting fat is ugly and unacceptable. Just ask twenty-year-old Amanda, who used to starve herself and even illegally bought ADHD meds from a guy in her dorm in order to suppress her appetite and slim down: "My freshman year of college, I started taking Adderall to curb my appetite, and I wouldn't eat for days. But I wasn't even worried about it. I just wanted to look good," she told me. "The only time I would eat would be when I didn't take a pill, and then I would binge on huge amounts of food. I knew something was wrong, but the sad thing is that I wasn't ashamed of my disordered eating habits until I started gaining weight. I liked not eating and how I looked; it was only when I started eating too much that I became ashamed and upset with myself.

Are All Bingers Overweight?

Not at all. This is a huge misperception that people have about emotional overeaters. I know people who have been reluctant to get help because they figure that if their body size is about right, their problem isn't "bad" enough to need fixing. "Believing your size is an indication of your mental or physical health is incorrect," said Dr. Nardozzi. "The extreme ends of eating disorders can lead to sizes that are way too small and too big. But what you really need to look at are your behaviors and your mind-set. Are you obsessing about food and your body? Is your mood affected by what you eat? Are you feeling bad about yourself for eating large amounts of food or are you restrictive with your eating after indulging? I've heard women at the Renfrew Center say, 'Oh God, I don't deserve to be here' because they don't think their bodies are sick enough. But are you having more days than not that you're feeling really awful about yourself and doing unhealthy behaviors? That's a better indicator of whether you have an eating problem than your weight alone."

When I was writing this book, I rented a desk in a little communal office space for writers in my neighborhood in Brooklyn so that I'd have a quiet place to work on the weekends. One day I was chatting with an older lady who asked what my project was about. When I said I was writing a book for girls who binge

eat, based partly on my own experience with binge eating disorder, she said, "Wow, really? You don't look like you binge." My
reply? "I'm recovered now. But it's funny you had that reaction:
Not all overeaters are overweight, and one reason I'm writing
the book is because there are so many misperceptions about
people like us."

I was significantly overweight at one time, though. When I
was twenty-two years old, during my short marriage while I was
in college, I weighed 225 pounds and was, according to body
mass index charts, clinically obese. Some emotional overeaters
are overweight or obese from the time they're children, but others yo-yo up and down, stay in a pretty normal range, or even
become underweight because of things like overexercising or
dieting. Kendra said she knows logically that her weight is normal, but she doesn't feel like it. "I weigh 123 pounds and I'm five
six, so technically I'm 'healthy,' but I don't feel healthy," she told
me. "I don't feel healthy unless I see definition in my abs and
weigh 112." (At 112 pounds, by the way, Kendra would be clinically underweight; just a few pounds from the official definition
of anorexic.) Twenty-one-year-old Sarah, on the other hand,
said she's always been on the larger side. "You could say that
I am morbidly obese, but I just say that I'm really overweight,"
she explained. "I'm only five two and weigh about 260 pounds.
I'm not comfortable in my body and always wear really baggy
clothes."

Weight fluctuations are incredibly common among overeaters. Amanda weighed just one hundred pounds after severely restricting herself in high school and her early college years— but she quickly put on forty pounds in one year once she started bingeing again. I've yo-yo'd, too. As an adult, I have been as slim as a size ten and as large as a size twenty. My weight is stable now and naturally fluctuates between five and ten pounds, depending on how active I've been and where I am in my menstrual cycle. The moral of these stories? Emotional overeaters come in all shapes and sizes.

Does Food Make You Miserable?

If you're reading this book, chances are there's something a little off about your relationship with food. Maybe you think about food all day long: what to eat, what not to eat, when you can eat, how much you can eat, how you can get exactly what you want to eat, if you should eat at all. Maybe you eat a lot of food, more than you think any normal person could possibly fit in their belly. Maybe you hide food under your bed, in your car, or in your desk drawer, because you feel panicky when you don't have snacks around—or because you don't want your roommate, parents, or significant other to know what you really eat, or how much of it. Maybe you consume whole boxes of cereal, pints of ice cream, or jars of peanut butter, and then stuff the containers deep in the trash so no one will know it was you who finished them off. Maybe you only ever eat when you're alone because you can't stand the thought of someone watching you do something so "shameful." Maybe you've taken food out of the garbage and eaten it, or eaten something that was burned or still frozen because you were desperate for it. Maybe you steal food from your family, roommates, coworkers, or even from the store. Maybe you make up excuses not to hang out with people so that you can go home and be alone with food. Maybe you've tried to make yourself throw up after a really big binge, or fasted to make up for it and promised yourself you'd never do it again.

Eating for psychological reasons, rather than from hunger, is called many things—binge eating disorder, EDNOS, emotional overeating, compulsive eating, binge eating, loss-of-control eating, food addiction, stress eating. And it can have many variations and levels of severity. You may find that you relate to one of these terms better than others, and I'll be telling the stories of girls and women who identify themselves in all of these different ways. For consistency's sake, I'm going to use the terms *binge eating* and *emotional overeating* in this book.

Whether you meet the criteria for an official eating disorder diagnosis or not, if your overeating and food obsession is causing you pain and problems in your life, you deserve to get better. Are you ready to start? Let's get to it!

Your Turn:

At the end of each chapter, I'll give you a few things to think about and write on, so grab some paper or a journal. These first three questions are meant to help you put down, in black and white, the things about your relationship with food that you may have been too afraid, or too ashamed, to admit before now. Know that whatever you write, you are not alone.

1. What is your weight and body history? Did you yo-yo like Amanda and I did? Are you slim but don't feel that way like Kendra, or do you struggle with being overweight or obese like Sarah?

2. Did you relate to any of the eating disorder descriptions in this chapter such as EDNOS or BED? How or why?

3. Do you think that you are an emotional overeater or binge eater? What terms would you use to describe your issues with food?

chapter two

Sound Familiar? A Few Things Emotional Overeaters Have in Common

remember walking into my first support group for overeaters when I was twenty-nine years old. I looked around at the people in the room and thought, *Wait... what?* These *women binge eat?* I don't know exactly what I was expecting, but what I found were girls of all ages, all cultures, and all sizes, some of whom were so put together and pretty that if I'd seen them on the street I would've been jealous!

I thought they were all so different from me, but sure enough, as these women raised their hands one by one and shared their stories, I was surprised to discover that I related to each and every one of them. Sure, the details were different, but our craziness about food and our bodies—and the way our brains worked and processed emotions like fear and anger—were shockingly similar. I learned two lessons that night that I will never ever forget: (1) You can't compare the way you feel on the inside to the way someone appears on the outside, and (2) No matter how different we may be as individuals, we emotional overeaters have a lot in common. As you read the things the girls in this chapter are talking about, keep this question in the back of your mind: Have you ever done, said, or thought anything like this?

Eating in Secret

It's almost universal: Every woman I've met at my support groups or talked to through HealthyGirl.org, my website for young women who emotionally overeat, has tried to keep the worst of their bingeing hidden from other people. That means bingeing in the middle of the night when our parents, roommates, or significant others are asleep; hiding food in our bedrooms, cars, or desk drawers; lying about food that "disappears" from the fridge; sometimes even stealing food when there's no other way to satisfy that overwhelming urge to eat. We feel ashamed about our behavior and take great pains to try to hide it from our family and friends—even waitresses or the people who work behind the counter at drugstores. It's not just the type or amount of food that is embarrassing; it's the fact that we have lost control. What we're doing with food feels disgusting and crazy, so why in the heck would we want anyone to know? Many of us go to great lengths to make sure nobody ever does.

"For me bingeing is such a secretive behavior, something I do in private that is my dirty little secret," Jenn, a twenty-one-year-old college student told me. "It's hard to do living at home since my eating habits are so scrutinized by my mother, but my recent binges all really have a few things in common: They take place in the afternoon or night, and no one else is around. If my parents are home, I wait until they are in bed, which is usually by nine, and binge in the basement while I watch TV." Like Jenn, I used to binge after my mom had gone to bed. I always kept the lights off in the kitchen, and usually turned on the water in the sink so she'd think I was just getting a drink. She did catch me once or twice—I remember her calling out from her bedroom, "Sunny? What are you doing?" The shame and embarrassment were almost unbearable.

Sometimes I'd binge on stuff while standing in front of the open fridge, but when I was too freaked about the possibility of my mom walking in, I'd grab cereal or crackers or whatever there was and hurry back to my room to eat it. The worst part of the deception would be waking up in the morning to the evidence: the crumbs, plates, bowls, or wrappers that littered the floor—sometimes even uneaten portions of food that I'd fallen asleep in the middle of chewing. I once woke up with half a piece of buttered bread next to my cheek on the pillow. As the realization of what I had done sank in, so would the self-hate and guilt.

Of course, we don't just binge in our kitchens or bedrooms. Some of us do it at work, school, even in our cars. "I do think at one point I had binge eating disorder," twenty-four-year-old Hillary told me. "I had always overeaten, but it got to a point in the last year or so when I knew it had spun out of control, when I would go out for a drive, order as much Taco Bell as possible, and then eat it in my car because I didn't want anybody to see." Dr. Bulik said that a lot of binge eaters do this very same thing. In fact, one of her fellow eating disorders researchers did a study to look at when and where people had the most "problematic eating episodes" and found that cars were one of the worst. I once downed twenty McDonald's Chicken McNuggets during a ride home after a disappointing trip to see a guy I had a crush on.

Another time, when I was nineteen, I binged in the parking lot of my diet doctor's office! I'd been seeing an expensive M.D. who had helped a friend of my mom's drop a bunch of weight with an all-protein diet, plus lots of horrible pills and weird bars. Part of the deal was that you had to go in once a week to be weighed and have your blood pressure taken. I was driving to the office for a weigh-in after about five weeks of deprivation on the diet when my hands just sort of steered me into a 7-Eleven parking lot. I felt like my mind just went blank, and kind of robotically, I walked in and bought a huge box of Dunkin'

Sticks glazed donut bars. As soon as I got back to the car I ripped the package open and started gobbling. I was finishing them up as I pulled up to the doctor's office, and I remember cramming the last one into my mouth and swallowing hard, forcing the dry, sugary dough down my throat before checking myself for crumbs and trudging inside.

Katrina, who's twenty-six and is expecting a baby with her husband, has binged in the car—and has also gone to great lengths to make sure her office mates don't find out about her on-the-job binges. "One thing I did a few months ago was buy brownies and cupcakes and other crap from the vending machines at work and go in the bathroom and eat it all in one of the stalls so my coworkers wouldn't see me," she told me. "I ate it fast, too, in case someone came in. It was gross and humiliating." Katrina no doubt feels like she's the only one who's ever gone so far as to eat in the loo, but other young women I talked to have resorted to doing it, too. Razieh (whom you met in Chapter 1) said that she knew she had a problem when she found herself locked in her parents' bathroom, shoving food into her mouth. Rachael, who's twenty, went so far as to bring a binge food into the shower with her: "I ate a block of chocolate in the bath," she told me. "Not wanting my mum to catch me and scared that she could hear me unwrapping the foil, I thought I would kill two birds with one stone: get clean, and binge. Although the hot water didn't help, and I found myself covered in sticky, runny chocolate."

Are bingers weak, disgusting, or gross?
No! We have a compulsion. A psychological
and physical urge so intense it feels as if we
simply cannot resist it.

It's probably safe to say that people who are normal about food wouldn't eat in the bathroom. But does that mean that we bingers are weak, disgusting, or "gross," as Katrina said she felt? No! It means that we have a compulsion—a psychological and physical urge so intense that it feels as if we simply cannot resist it. The compulsion to eat (and eat and eat) is so strong that we will do whatever it takes to get the food into our bodies. "Right before I binge, I feel extremely paranoid," said sixteen-year-old Bobbie. "I run over all the thoughts in my head about why one binge will not hurt, and how it will make me happy. All that matters is the food."

Lying About What We Eat

Something we emotional overeaters or bingers must often do in order to keep our secret is lie—to ourselves, to our friends and loved ones, even to strangers. "In my twenties, I used to order extra drinks so that the fast-food employees, who do not know me and will never know me, would not judge me," Heather, who's now thirty-two, told me. "Same thing in bakeries. I would order a dozen or more items and make a comment about how my fake husband or family were waiting at home for me to bring the dessert. It's crazy. Truly crazy." Well, it may not be "normal," but it's something a whole lot of young women have done. "A normal person can go into a restaurant and order whatever they want and not think anything about it or feel judged," said twenty-two-year-old Isabel. "I felt I always had eyes on me, that the person behind the register was judging me. So I'd walk into the restaurant on my cell phone, stand to the side looking up at the menu, and talk to myself. Or rather, to the 'friend' I was taking an order from. Of course, I already knew what I wanted. I'd order up to three different meals at a time, each with a different drink, but they were all for me. The food was like a reward for cleverly deceiving everyone present at the restaurant. It's amazing some of the things we do to maintain this lifestyle."

While I didn't lie to servers or cashiers, I did lie about what I ate, mostly by omission. When I was in my late teens, very depressed, and bingeing almost nightly, food would "disappear" from our fridge on a regular basis. My mother and I both knew where the food was going (into my mouth), but we didn't openly talk about it. I was so sensitive about food and my weight that she began to avoid the subject at all costs. Instead, she created a story about a gnome who would break into the house at night and gobble up all our food. She'd head to the kitchen and look for the crackers or cheese or whatever, and when she realized they were gone, she'd say, "Well, that damn gnome must've struck again!" Somehow that story let me know that she knew what I was going through, but that she didn't want to interfere. After lots of fights and teary talks, she knew I had to deal with it in my own time and in my own way.

My sneaking around and lying continued when I moved out of the house and got roommates in my early twenties. Sometimes, when the urge to binge would strike, I'd steal their food or finish off a box of shared cereal or loaf of bread. To keep them from finding out, I'd bury the empty packages deep in the trash can, run out and buy a replacement, and then either throw some away or eat it back down to the level it was before. (Replacing leftover Chinese takeout or half-eaten cheeseburgers was harder to do. I knew I couldn't cover up what I'd done, so I would make something up about being drunk and having the munchies.)

Most of us have had to work pretty hard to hide the evidence of what we do with food when no one's looking. "I live on my own now and have for many years," said Shannon, who is twenty-six. "So at home, it's easy to binge and not have anyone to justify my behavior or the missing food to. However, when I'm expecting visitors or out visiting, I do tend to hide evidence of my consumption. I bury packages at the bottom of the garbage bin, rearrange cookies so it looks like I ate fewer than I actually took, or simply switch the food I'm eating so I've eaten a little of a lot of different things instead of a lot of one thing."

This fear and obsession around hiding the evidence is often magnified when we're trying to keep this a secret from someone we're dating. "When I was in college, I often hid the bags from fast-food restaurants from my boyfriend," said twenty-three-year-old Amy. "He was a personal trainer and was very vocal about not wanting to date a 'fat girl.' I still instinctively hide wrappers from fast-food places in the trash can, even though my husband doesn't care at all what I eat, and I know he wouldn't mind me eating fast food."

Vowing to Start Over

Of course, after a big binge, many of us vow it'll never happen again. "I promised myself that by my eighteenth birthday I would be back to my old healthy self and would never use food as a comfort again," Kendra told me. "But I realize now that maybe that promise was just a reason to change my obsession from bingeing to restricting. Now, whenever I eat a carbohydrate like cereal, I feel guilty and figure I might as well binge on whatever else I can get my hands on. My brain shuts off all reasoning and logic. Then I start over the next day."

When I was fourteen or fifteen, before my mom and I put a moratorium on food talk, we would go on diets together. I wasn't overweight yet, and she's never been fat, but we still somehow thought we needed to drop pounds. One of us would "blow it" (her term, which I hated), and we'd look at each other and say, like an echo, "It's okay, we'll start our diets tomorrow ... tomorrow ... tomorrow ... tomorrow." That "I'll start over tomorrow" thinking lasted through my teens and midtwenties. After a weekend of bingeing, I'd tell myself that I would start over on Monday. I'd somehow overcome the emotional overeating through sheer force of will—and then I'd get thin and everything would be perfect.

Yeah, well, that didn't happen (and the whole thin-equals-perfect thing is, of course, a big, fat myth). Without addressing the underlying compulsion and emotions that were driving me to eat in the first place, I simply wasn't able to stop. Kendra sums it up perfectly: "It's so exhausting! Food, something so simple and so controllable, is controlling me. Every minute of every day I'm calculating my day's worth of calories, and how many I have left to eat, or how many hours of exercise I need to burn off what I binged on. I'm tired of food being the center of my life. It's become my comfort and my biggest fear all at once."

The end result of all this promise breaking is that we begin to see ourselves as being untrustworthy, unreliable. We don't do what we say we're going to do—and that breaks down our self-image and self-esteem. How can you feel good about being a person who can't seem to keep a promise? Too bad we're giving ourselves impossible promises to keep.

Eating Crazy Stuff

Sometimes the craving for certain foods—usually sweets or fatty things for me—takes you to places you never thought you'd go. Like the trash can. "The other night I was home alone and bored and stressed," Shannon told me. "So I ordered a pizza and, as I was putting the order through, realized I wanted fries, too. And when the delivery guy came, the box was huge, enough for a family. I ate the entire small pizza and most of the box of fries. Then I threw all the trash from the meal on top of the leftovers and put it on the kitchen counter to toss in the morning, and waddled off to bed so full I felt like I was going to throw up. The next morning I woke up, took the box of fries off the counter, took the garbage—dirty napkins, empty dip containers—off the top and ate the rest of the fries. When I finished I was so disgusted and ashamed of myself and so happy that I lived alone and no one could see my habits."

Well, Shannon's not the only one who's brushed aside a little garbage in order to satisfy the urge to eat. "Last night I bought a tub of low-fat ice cream thinking I would have two scoops," Rachael said. "I ended up eating half the tub in one sitting. I threw the rest into the trash, but when I went to the fridge and there was nothing 'bad' to eat, I went to the bin, found the tub, and finished it off."

I've done it, too—more than once. I'd eat half of something and then bury the rest in the garbage thinking that would stop me from eating any more of it. But if the compulsion to binge was strong enough, not even garbage would stop me.

"When I binge, I tend to do so with carb-rich, sweet foods," Shannon told me. "I've known myself to eat entire batches of raw cookie dough and huge pans of corn bread, with a quarter pound of butter smeared on the pieces. I've also eaten a loaf of bread in one sitting, going back to make toast with butter and cinnamon or butter and brown sugar. On more than one occasion, I've caught myself eating out of the garbage can or eating so much that I find myself throwing up. I don't make myself throw up, but rather the sheer volume of food that I've inhaled is more than my body can handle."

The urge to eat something "bad" is something else a lot of us share. I don't know about you, but stuffing myself with oatmeal or fruit just never seemed to hit that emotional spot like a bucket of buttery popcorn, spoonfuls of pure frosting, or something else I thought of as naughty. "When there aren't any foods my brain considers bad enough, I will make my own concoctions," Rachael told me. "For example, I would take bread, slather it in butter, put fatty salad dressing on it, baked beans, nuts, tomato, ham, three types of cheese, and whack it all together and chow down. When I told a friend of mine about it, she said, 'But weren't you sick?' The sad thing is, I wasn't. That was just a minibinge. After I do something like that and 'ruin' the day, I can continue, sometimes for hours. And it's only after I am so bloated, gassy, and have a migraine that I will actually stop eating."

My own binge concoctions usually centered around sweets. I once melted sugar and Kool-Aid powder in a nonstick frying pan to make candy. I ate peanut butter with granulated sugar, maple syrup, or Karo corn syrup poured on top. I made home-made frosting from powered sugar and butter. Once, my craving for something sweet pushed me to mix shredded coconut, cocoa powder, sugar, and peanut butter in a bowl and eat it like raw cookie dough.

Choosing Food over People

When I was in my early twenties, in the worst throes of my binge eating disorder, the compulsion to eat was so strong that I would turn down invitations to go out so that I could stay home and eat. I was so lonely back then, but the urge to binge was stronger than the urge to connect with other people. Other times I'd hurry a friend, or even a date, out the door so I could be alone and raid the cupboards. Rachael had similar experiences: "I used to wish my beautiful boyfriend would leave my house so that I could eat everything in the fridge. I would rather sit and stuff my face with ice cream and sandwiches than hang out, have fun, or make love."

"One client I worked with compared the eating disorder she had to a really bad boyfriend," said Dr. Nardozzi. "That boyfriend who is really controlling and wants all your time and doesn't want you to be with your friends. The food obsession can take up a lot of space within somebody and it doesn't feel like there's a lot of room for other things. For some people it may be work that suffers, for other it's school or other activities. All these behaviors have the effect of making you miss out on life." Sometimes you just want to isolate yourself because you want to be with the food and in your funk, she said, but other times it's deeper than that. "I have a client who avoids her family because she feels like they now know too much about her treatment for her eating disorder, and that if she's around them and they see her behaving strangely at all with food, they might call her out," Dr. Nardozzi told me. "She thinks people aren't going to get what she's going through. I also hear women say they don't want to have to go to an event where there's a buffet, or they don't want to go to a party because they don't have clothes that fit them. I'm seeing one woman right now who has had a lot of weight gain and she's just so uncomfortable being

---

The food obsession can take up a lot of
space within somebody and it doesn't feel
like there's a lot of room for other things.
For some people it may be work that suffers,
for other it's school or other activities. All
these behaviors have the effect of making
you miss out on life.

---

out in public. Her weight gain was really quick, so she wants to hide."

This acute awareness of and obsession with our bodies are things binge eaters tend to have in common. "I try to avoid dinners out, especially parties with open tables of snacks or buffets because I feel so embarrassed about the sheer volume of food I can put away," said Shannon. "I'm not a small person, I'm five seven and wear a size fourteen, and sometimes feel like I'm going to be judged. You know, 'That girl could afford to lose a few pounds, why is she loading up on cheese and crackers?' Besides that, I find social events that revolve around food simply un-fun. I spend the evening obsessing about how much I want to eat that entire bowl of chips that I don't get to enjoy the company of the people around me."

If I had to count the number of times I canceled plans or blew off a party because I had binged or felt too fat to go anywhere I would have to pull out a calculator and do some of that exponential math that I learned in Algebra II. It's something about me that I don't think anyone—from high school friends to my BFF since first grade, Cheri—would ever have guessed. I've always been popular enough, outgoing, funny, cheerful, a life-of-the-party type. But truthfully, sometimes I would get so wrapped up in my insecurities that I felt deathly afraid of being around people. When these moods would hit and I was already out with friends, I would feel like I was standing out somewhere in the stratosphere just observing. Watching them have fun. Watching them flirt, watching them being natural and funny. Watching them seem so . . . comfortable. All the while I'd be wondering if everyone could tell that I was freaking out, or thinking my belly looked big, or about how I could feel back fat blorping out from under my bra strap.

I used to feel guilty about all the "missing out" I did. Guilty that I wasted so many nights alone at home when I could've been connecting with people I like or love. But all those times I isolated or skipped out on people in order to be alone and binge, I wasn't choosing food over friends. I was actually kind of choosing myself. I was trying to soothe and take care of myself; I just didn't know the right way to do it. These days I don't look back with disgust or judgment on any of the bingeing, sneaking around, or isolating I did. I look back with compassion for a girl who was very confused, very sad, and had little control over her actions. I hope you can do the same.

Your Turn:

You already know what weird things you may do with food, but these three journaling topics from Jennifer Nardozzi, Psy.D., are meant to help you begin to discover why you do them.

1. It may seem like your eating habits are the problem, but they're just a symptom of what's really going on. How does food serve your deeper needs? Do you use it to soothe pain, for example? Or to protect yourself from uncomfortable social situations?

2. Food is often a metaphor for something else, like a reward or a vacation. "Each person has a very different metaphor," said Dr. Nardozzi. "One woman I'm working with is a student who also has many other projects that she is managing simultaneously. She's so busy, but the binges make everything stop. It's how she gets a break." What does food mean to you?

3. Many disordered eaters feel a lot of guilt for their bingeing or emotional eating. How can you start to forgive yourself and replace judgment with understanding and compassion?

chapter three

Oh, So *That's* How We Got This Way

've always been a writer. In fact, I wrote my very first poem at
the age of six. It sounds kind of cute and precocious until you
hear what it was about: a diet. That's right; the first bit of creative writing my little brain ever churned out was about food. I
still know it by heart:

> There once was a mouse named Cheesy
> Who saw some Limburger cheese.
> He said, "I can't eat that, I'm on a diet.
> I'd rather have some peas!"

How the heck did I even know what a diet was back then?
Or that cheese was more fattening than vegetables? Once I

started taking a closer look at my family and childhood, it started to make sense. In this chapter, we'll explore some of the things that may have contributed to your issues with food.

Your Genes

For some of us, food and eating problems start really, really early. We're talking the womb. "Genetics play a huge role in eating disorders; a girl whose mother has binge eating disorder, bulimia, or anorexia is at a higher risk of it herself," said Dr. Sophy. One study of nine hundred people found that a person is twice as likely to binge eat if he or she has a relative who also has the disorder. Another found that if a person's parent had binge eating disorder, they had a 57 percent chance of having it, too. The fact is, lots of research has found that binge eating disorder—as well as other eating disorders and even preoccupation with weight and negative body image—tend to run in familes.

They sure seemed to run in mine. My dad used to get up often in the middle of the night and eat ice cream. That's not too weird, lots of dads might do that—but he would also sometimes eat a can of frozen orange juice concentrate with a spoon, straight out of the container. That's a little weirder, right? (And, like I mentioned earlier, frozen orange juice was exactly what I chose to eat during one of my first binges.) A couple of years ago, when I went home for Christmas, I commented on how good he looked—nice and strong and sort of bulky, like he'd been putting on muscle weight. He said, "Really? Must be all the peanut butter I'm stress-eating." He'd been having a tough time getting to sleep and dealing with my wonderful—but very active and precocious—six-year-old twin sisters, and had apparently been shoveling in the PB in order to help himself calm down at night. Interestingly, peanut butter has always been one of my go-to binge foods, too.

Rachael believes she may have inherited some of her disordered eating tendencies. "When I told my mum about my binge eating disorder, she empathized and told me that when she was in high school, she used to binge," she said. "And I think my dad binge eats. He weighs nearly 220 pounds and smokes pot, and so I notice he gorges on food late at night when he has the

---

Binge eating disorder—as well as other eating disorders and even preoccupation with weight and negative body image— tends to run in familes.

---

munchies. He can easily eat a half-pound bar of chocolate in one night without thinking about it. He started keeping the junk food in his room when I asked him to get rid of it, but then he complained it was making him feel uncomfortable eating in his room, in secret, like a dirty habit."

Your Family's Economic Situation

What the heck does money have to do with your food and body issues? It's actually pretty simple. Financial problems can cause a lot of stress, and if our parents were stressed, there's no doubt that we picked up on it. A recent study from the University of Illinois actually found that kids from poorer families tend to reach for "comfort foods" like sweets and other junky stuff when they're feeling anxious. Almost 40 percent of the children and teens in the study were found to be either overweight or obese— a higher rate than the national average of around 33 percent. "When I was a kid, I used to sneak into the kitchen late at night or when everyone else was occupied and raid the cookie jar," Shannon told me. "I grew up in a home where every penny had to be stretched. I never went without, but those cookies were for school lunches. I would eat dozens in one sitting. Then I would steal from my mom's purse or, as I got older, use my own money to replace the cookies that I ate." Sarah thinks money still plays into her overeating behavior. "I'm a broke college student and my mom still supports me. We don't have much money, so I don't really get to eat much throughout the day," she explains. "I usually just eat dinner and then some junk food. I notice that when I do get the opportunity to eat, I eat my food really fast. When I'm done eating I sit there wondering 'Where did my food go?'"

Part of this food-money connection could also be a fear of not having enough, said Dr. Sophy. If you don't know when you're going to have access to food, you're going to eat as much of it as you possibly can when you do have access to it. "It's fear-based. Whether it's fear of abandonment or fear of not having enough. A lack of financial resources only adds another intense layer." Not only that, but when you grow up living in a lower-income neighborhood, you tend to have fewer healthy food choices nearby. If you're surrounded by McDonald's and KFC, it's easy—and cheap—to binge on fries or popcorn chicken when the urge hits you. It's a big problem, and some city and state governments are even getting involved trying to limit the number of fast-food restaurants that can be in certain neighborhoods. That doesn't solve the problem of candy being thrown in your face at every 7-Eleven and front counter of every drugstore, but some experts say it's a start.

Your Family Traditions

A lot of us got the idea growing up that food was the answer for all kinds of things: a reward, a celebration, comfort. When you're a baby, of course, you get milk or food when you cry, or to help you go to sleep. But using food for comfort like that doesn't always end when we grow up. I remember one New Year's Eve my brother and sister were at a church party and my mom and dad were going to a family friend's house. I was old enough to stay home alone for a few hours, but my mom felt so guilty about leaving me that she let me watch TV in her room and tucked me into her bed with a Big Mac, fries, and a strawberry shake. She knew being surrounded by food would make me happy; and it did! But it may have set a bad precedent.

My parents also used to take me to the all-you-can-eat buffet at Sizzler after my piano recitals. It was sweet, it was a tradition, it felt good, but sadly, it reinforced something already inside me that was predisposed to have an unhealthy relationship with food. I really did start to associate food with doing a good job. French fries, or candy, or chips, or whatever became like a prize. Anytime anything good happened for me or I succeeded at something, I'd instantly want to reward myself or celebrate with food.

For a lot of people, celebrations center completely around

food. Think of Thanksgiving, for goodness' sake! That's an entire day dedicated, in most families, to eating so much you have to unbutton your pants. Food sometimes feels like family itself. "Coming from an Iranian family, like any big family full of tradition, food of course is the epicenter of our life," Razieh told me. "Every time my family gets together—which is every Sunday night for dinner—my mother prepares a large Iranian feast. Food is what brings us together. Not eating everything on your plate is basically a sin and in fact an insult to the host. This has definitely been one of the biggest challenges with my eating disorder. I honestly feel guilty when I don't eat a lot, but at the same time do experience trouble stopping other times. Sometimes I think, 'If I'm gonna binge, its best to do it here, that way at least I will be making Mommy happy.'"

"In some cultures, food is love and comfort; in others, you're taught as a woman to provide the food, not eat it," said Dr. Sophy. "I've seen in my patients that in some male-focused cultures, women often serve and then sit back. You should cook and provide and nurture and not always partake. You partake later. What a great way to rebel—to overpartake."

Your Mom's Relationship with Food and Her Body

My mother came from a long line of pretty (and skinny) women. In her family, looks meant a lot. My gorgeous and glamorous grandmother Ruth dated movie stars and stole men from their wives. One aunt competed in beauty pageants. My mom modeled bikinis when she was eighteen and living in Hawaii. The highest compliment you could get in her family was that you looked beautiful and thin. I remember one Christmas Day my grandfather got a newfangled digital bathroom scale as a gift, and he made my mom and all her sisters step on it in the middle of the living room. In front of everyone. Then he said things like "That's my beautiful daughter!" or "Whoa, you're packing on pounds!" and even "Oh, you're too skinny!" It was humiliating for my mother and her sisters, and it scared me to death. I was relieved that my cousins and I were too young to be scrutinized just yet.

My mother never developed a full-blown eating disorder of her own, but she admits now that she's always been a little weird about food. Even though she was slim, we always had calorie-counting books around the house when I was growing up and she used to go on strange juicing kicks or do salad-and-bread-only diets to lose a few pounds before summers on the beach. She definitely passed some of that focus on weight to me. When I was fourteen and a sophomore in high school (I had skipped a grade), I was nominated for homecoming princess. My mom bought me a long red satin gown with a sweetheart neckline, spaghetti straps, and sparkly crystals in the front. I loved it. It fit, but was a little tight around the tummy. We could've gone to a dry cleaner or tailor to have the dress altered, but she got me a gym membership instead. (I still remember the personal trainer who showed me around the gym looking at us like we were crazy when my mom explained that we just wanted me to lose three or four pounds before homecoming.)

Considering that our parents pretty much teach us how to live for the first years of our lives, it's no surprise that whatever issues they have about food and weight trickle down to us. "It's not just in the genes they pass down," said Dr. Sophy. "Our parents' attitudes about food and weight and their own eating habits have an incredible influence on every one of us."

I not only learned how to diet from my mom, I may have—at least partially—learned about bingeing from her, too. Based on what phase my mom was in at the time, our family would go from being totally vegetarian health nuts for a month or two to ordering pizza and eating huge desserts. One of the family favorites when Mom was in "eating" mode was vanilla ice cream with Cap'n Crunch cereal and hot coffee poured on top. I remember we used to eat it out of silver mixing bowls. It was like Goldilocks and the bears or something; my dad would get the biggest one, my mom would get the medium one, and me and my brother and sister would get the smaller ones. I loved these family-style junk-food pig-out sessions at the time. But, not surprisingly, they warped my understanding of what normal portions were—and made me subconsciously feel that eating a lot meant fun, family, and comfort.

Some of us may have followed the example of overeating parents; but sometimes bingeing and overeating can develop because we want to rebel against our parents' values, said Dr. Sophy. "Hiding food from your family, eating things you're not 'supposed to' or getting fat in a thin family can be a way to set yourself apart, to rebel against the rules and culture in your house," he said. For "good girls," eating things you know your mom wouldn't approve of, in amounts she definitely wouldn't approve of, is such an easy (and safe) way to disobey. "You get fat in a family that really cares about thinness and it's like you're flipping them off," said Dr. Sophy. And, unlike drugs or alcohol, food is readily available from the time we're little kids, and it's perfectly legal.

Take the story of one of Dr. Sophy's Beverly Hills clients, a

_____

Our parents' attitudes about food and weight and their own eating habits have an incredible influence on every one of us.

_____

seventeen-year-old we'll call Lily. Her parents were super-high profile—her mom was a model, her dad was a high-powered business type. All of a sudden, Lily started bingeing like crazy, and her parents didn't know what to do. "I went out to dinner with them as a family several times just to observe," Dr. Sophy told me. "Mom would comment on her daughter's choices at every meal. She'd say, 'Don't order that, it's fattening.' They'd leave that restaurant and the girl would feel horrible. Guilty about ordering the bad stuff, and then really angry at her mom." Lily was eating out of anger and rebellion. Dr. Sophy worked with her for about seven months to help her discover other ways to deal with her anxiety and anger, and he worked with Lily's mom, too. "I taught her that she couldn't inflict her own body image and eating issues on her daughter like that," he said.

Jenn, now twenty-one, recalls that things her mother said made her self-conscious about her weight at a very young age. "I remember always being aware of my size as a child—and being told by my mom in the fifth grade that I didn't fit into the Lands' End children's clothing anymore. She showed me a chart that said that the kids size sixteen was supposed to fit a fourteen-year-old. When I was in middle school, the low-carb craze was big and she told me that all I needed to do to keep my weight in check was to monitor my carbs."

Hillary strongly believes her mom has influenced her relationship with food, as well. "It's been pretty clear to me that her insecurity with her own body has been transferred over to me," she said. "I've always felt like the chubby girl, but when I look back on photos I can't believe that I ever thought that. No one ever made fun of me for being fat and it's pretty clear to me now that it was all in my head. I really think this came from believing that my mom thought I was fat. I've always loved food and always ate pretty quickly, so the comments that came from my mother about the way I ate or telling me what I should and shouldn't be eating just made me go crazy."

I can relate: I always felt like my mom thought I was fat, too. Remember those calorie-counting books of hers? Well, when I was about nine years old, I started playing around with them, experimenting to see just how few calories I could eat in a day. Once I logged just eight hundred—and when I excitedly told her about it, she said, "That's good, Sunny!" Looking back, I realize that if she had been thinking clearly, or healthily, she would've said something more like "What the heck are you doing counting calories?" or "That's not enough—open your mouth and eat this sandwich!"

I wasn't exactly overweight, but I was solidly built and I think my mother was a little afraid of my appetite. She must have seen inklings of my predisposition for binge eating. After all, she had witnessed me putting away three hot dogs with the works as a toddler, and once I even grabbed a stick of butter off the table and started licking it like a lollipop. My mother admits she really didn't want me to get fat. She always said it was because she didn't want me to struggle or be in pain; but I also believe part of it was because she was taught that fat was ugly. Remember, she grew up in a family that was incredibly focused on looks and thinness. She had always been valued almost exclusively for her good looks; her intelligence, sensitivity, and creativity were completely ignored. But she was praised constantly for being thin and pretty.

Hillary's mom didn't want her to get big, either. "Although my mom has always made little comments, they became more hurtful as I gained more weight," she said. "One thing she said that really hurt me was 'I don't think you can ever be happy as long as you're overweight.' It made me feel as though she thought I didn't deserve to be happy unless I lost weight. She could never feel happy while she was fat, so I think she can't understand why anyone else would. I wish she could've told me that she'd love me no matter what weight I was and just wanted me to be happy and healthy. It's taken me a long time to tell her that these things hurt my feelings—where before I used to just scream and yell at her. It's caused a lot of tension in our relationship over the years, and I truly hope that things will get better now that she knows I have a disorder and am getting help for it."

I used to be pretty angry with my mother for the not-so-great lessons about body image and food that I learned from watching her. But the truth is, she had no idea how her issues and actions would combine with my personality and predispositions toward eating problems. And I'm not angry anymore. She honestly didn't know any better at the time—to be fair, no one even knew there was such a thing as binge eating disorder in the 1980s and '90s. Heck, anorexia and bulimia were barely even talked about. She did the best she could with the internal and external resources she had at the time.

Luckily, as we grow up, we have the chance to rid ourselves of any lessons we've learned that do more harm than good. You don't have to live with these food and body issues forever, or pass them along to your own children down the line. Breaking the cycle starts now.

Your Turn:

It can be incredibly helpful to have an idea of how your food issues began. "If you know which events, traditions, or family beliefs contributed to your disorder, you can go back and start to change the way you think about those things and replace the hurtful behaviors with more healthy ones," said Dr. Sophy. These questions are meant to help get you there.

1. Do your mom, dad, or other family members diet constantly, binge, or have other strange eating habits? Are they overweight? Underweight?

2. What does food mean in your family? Did it mean fun, love, reward, celebration? How do you think this may have affected your emotional overeating?

3. What's your earliest memory of weight or body worries?

4. What's your earliest memory of a "binge"? What happened, what did you eat, and how did you feel afterward?

5. Does your father or mother bad-mouth his or her body—or yours? How does that make you feel, and what has that taught you about the importance of body size to your self-worth?

part two:
let the healing begin!
how to start getting sane about food

chapter four

It's Not About the Food: What the Real Problem Is, and How to Fix It

I n the last few chapters, I talked a lot about things that emotional overeaters and bingers tend to do: Many of us eat in secret, yo-yo diet, isolate, make weird food concoctions, lie about what we eat, even eat out of the trash. Those actions and habits are clearly problematic. But you know what? They aren't the problem. Emotional overeating, binge eating, and other types of disordered eating aren't about food at all. "Food obsession and weight issues are just a consequence of whatever else you're really hungry for," said Jennifer Nardozzi, Psy.D. "If you keep focusing on the symptom, you're missing it. If you go on a diet and lose a few pounds, you're just putting a Band-Aid on it."

So if food isn't the real issue, what is? The full picture is complicated and different for each one of us, but the three components I want to focus on here are these:

- Our self-esteem

- Our black-and-white thinking

- Traumatic experiences in our pasts

It's understandable why many of us start our recovery journey believing that if we can just stop the bingeing and maintain a comfortable body size, we'll be fine. Those things are tangible, easy to understand, and, ostensibly, controllable—while the actual driving forces beneath our overeating are more amorphous, painful, and honestly, a little scary. Some of you might be cringing right now, and even wondering if you can skip ahead and just do without this part. But stick with me on this—I know you have the courage to dip into the real stuff. You might shed a couple of tears during this chapter, but you'll be so glad you did.

What's Self-Esteem Got to Do with It?

No one who knows me would guess that it's taken me years to feel worthy of being happy and healthy. If you'd asked me when I was twenty-five years old if I had a "self-esteem" problem, I would've laughed. Me? Low self-esteem? Please. I knew that I was at least somewhat talented since I was getting hired for jobs and freelance writing gigs. I had friends. I dated regularly. Plus, look how driven I was! Friends from high school and college would talk with a bit of awe about how I had moved three thousand miles away from California to New York City and landed a job at a major magazine. People from back home told me it looked like I was "living the dream." I was confident on the outside, but deep inside, when people would say things like that, I'd think, *Oh really? What dream is that? The one where I'm constantly anxious and beating myself up for little mistakes? The one in which if I'm not perfect, I'm garbage?* Those of us who deal with secret eating issues can often feel like frauds. "Even if everything looks great from the outside, we know things are not as they should be," Rebecca Radcliffe, an expert on body image, eating, and women's issues, told me.

Even as a very little girl, I never felt like I was as smart or as good as I should be. I remember feeling incredibly guilty for normal little-kid naughtiness like giggling when someone poked fun at another kid, or for not wanting to share. I once felt compelled to pick up trash around the playground at recess because I thought it was the "right" thing to do—and you had to always do the correct thing if you wanted to be acceptable and loved, didn't you? I thought I could and should be perfect; and when I fell short of that in any way, I felt like dirt. I had somehow gotten the message that I needed to be perfect in order to be worthy of acceptance, love, happiness, and success. Some of those beliefs may have stemmed from my family's religion (a pretty strict Protestant Christian denomination), or perhaps I was influenced by high standards set by my parents. I was a smart kid, and they strongly encouraged me to achieve. I was supersensitive to their expectations, internalizing them and giving them a lot of power over my own feelings. Despite the fact that my parents told me often that they loved me or that I did a good job, something in me still did not feel like I was enough.

It could be that a self-esteem-crumbling focus on perfection is something we are just born with: Research has shown that a tendency toward perfectionism is incredibly common among people with eating disorders of all kinds and that there may be a genetic component. The really awful thing about perfectionism is that it constantly erodes your self-esteem even further. "It's a line of thinking we call expecting perfection," said Cynthia Bulik, Ph.D. "You may feel that anything less than excellence means failure and it reflects upon your worth as a person."

Do You Expect Perfection?

Perfectionism is the mistaken belief that not only is it *possible* for you to perform perfectly at work, in school, in relationships, and in life, but also that people *expect* you to. If you agree with any of these statements, said Dr. Bulik, you may be perfectionistic:

1. Falling short of a goal often makes you think, *I'm a failure*, not just, *I failed.*
2. You set a goal, achieve it, then tell yourself it was no big deal and set the goal higher.
3. You do something 99 percent right, and all you can focus on is the 1 percent that was wrong.

Bottom line: Perfectionism is a lie. It is physically and mentally impossible for any human being to be perfect. (Not only that, but since our ideas of "perfect" vary, there isn't even one ideal to strive toward.) The next time the perfectionist in you says you're not good enough, ask yourself why, logically, you should be expected to do, be, look, or act more "perfectly" than anyone else. If someone at some point in your life told you that you had to be perfect in order to be loved, they were wrong.   ✳

Since no human can possibly be perfect, the perfectionist constantly fails. Failure makes us feel sad, disappointed, guilty, and bad about ourselves, and the thing we use to cope with and soothe those feelings—food—makes us feel like even more of a loser. "I think my biggest source of shame is simply the fact that I see binge eating disorder as a sign of weakness," said Shannon. "I'm a single, fiercely independent woman who views myself as strong and self-sufficient. And I'm proud of those things. But when I think about my relationship with food, it feels like an area of my life in which I've failed. The fact that I'm not coping as well as I should be coping is a sign of weakness, which makes me feel ashamed. I don't like asking for help because I don't like the connotation that it means that I can't do it all alone."

Shannon thinks she *should* be able to cope better. *Should* be able to do it alone. Should, should, should! If there was one word in the whole English language that Dr. Bulik would like to ban, it's that one. "Think about it," she said: "Would someone with diabetes say to themselves, 'My pancreas *should* be able to produce insulin'? Of course not! But with psychological symptoms—all of which have biological roots or correlates—we have this fantasy that we should be able to pull ourselves up by the bootstraps and not be depressed or anxious, binge or restrict. Shoulds are torture, and they typically come from some unrealistic external standard. Sometimes it's a cultural or societal myth like 'Women shouldn't eat a lot in public,' or 'Mothers should stay at home with their children.'"

> ### exericse:
> ## what are your "shoulds"?

An important step in letting go of unrealistic expectations is to pinpoint and examine which "shoulds" you have bought into, said Dr. Bulik. Grab your journal, a piece of paper, or your laptop. This exercise will take about ten minutes. Feel free to come back and do it again anytime you find yourself feeling bad about yourself.

- First, make a list of some of the things you think you should look like, be like, and be able to do.

- For each of your "shoulds," write down where you learned that it was important. Was it from watching your sister, your friends, or your favorite TV show? Did an ex-boyfriend, teacher, or your parents tell you it was required? Do these "shoulds" come from your voice? Do they come from someone else's voice that you have internalized?

- Next, ask yourself why you believe it's important to look or be that way, or do those things. What will being or doing those things get you in life: Love? Acceptance? Friends? Approval? Success? Do you think they will help your self-esteem?

- Lastly, ask yourself what would happen if you didn't try to look, be, or do these "shoulds." This last step is where many of us stumble upon some real core issues—for me, many of my "shoulds" boiled down to a fear of being abandoned, rejected, or not being loved.

Bottom line: "'Shoulds' are destructive and disrespectful to the self, and ultimately they are not motivating," said Dr. Bulik. The emotional consequence of these beliefs is unhealthy guilt and eroded self-worth. But things can change, with awareness and conscious effort. When I make a mistake now—whether it has to do with food, work, or relationships with friends and family—I no longer angrily (and abusively!) tell myself I should've done something different. I accept it, forgive myself if necessary, then think about how I might be able to deal with the next situation more healthfully or effectively.

What do all of our "shoulds" and self-worth issues have to do with overeating? I believe that fragile self-esteem—whether it's caused by perfectionism, genetics, or anything else—translates into overeating in a few ways. First, of course, many of us use food to take the edge off the painful feelings of self-hate and disappointment. As you know, food distracts and soothes us in the moment, but it ends up backfiring: "Binge eating makes me feel terrible about myself, which makes me binge eat more to deal with the bad feelings," said Shannon. "It's a never-ending cycle." Here's a connection that's perhaps not quite as obvious: Food also provides an incredibly convenient excuse if we do fail at something. "I have used my body and weight as a safety net or excuse for so many things—just a blanket reason in case I failed: 'Well, it's because I'm a binge eater' or 'I'm too big to do that,'" said Rachael.

When I was in my midtwenties, the eating allowed me to accept and explain why I wasn't thriving at work. I'd gone from being incredibly driven when I first moved to New York City to being a bit fatalistic and depressed: "I can't meet my deadlines because I'm too busy obsessing about food and my body to concentrate." That was partly true, but I also had some time management habits that could've used a little work. I would also tell myself, "I shouldn't even try to get a promotion because I'm always late to work. And I'm late because I'm hungover from bingeing the night before." It's true that I was often "hungover" from food and would wake up with heartburn, a bloated belly, and a clouded mind. But the real reason I was late for work, procrastinated on projects, or self-sabotaged in myriad other ways is that I was afraid to do well. If I rose up the ranks, if I really soared, if I gained more respect from my bosses and colleagues, it would set the bar too high. I didn't believe that I was actually good, talented, or strong enough to maintain success. I figured that even if I succeeded at first, I'd eventually fail.

This is perhaps the biggest benefit that binge eating gives to those of us with fragile self-worth: It gives us an excuse for not trying, for not even putting ourselves out there in the first place. It's a concept that Morgan, a twenty-two-year-old recovered binge eater, describes as using food to take yourself out of the game. "It's an idea I have gone back to multiple times in my recovery," she said. "Sometimes I think it is really easy to use food, weight, and body hatred as a shield to take myself out of the game without even thinking about it. It could be the social game, the relationship game, the employment game, the taking-a-risk game, the buying-pretty-new-clothes game, the list goes on and on. It's a protective measure perhaps gone too far. In a way, it's safe and easy, but it also causes a lot of pain and suffering as well."

It's clear that self-esteem issues are harmful to us and help perpetuate our overeating and bingeing. So, how do we fix them? "We don't understand self-esteem well at all," said psychologist Michael Lukens, Ph.D., clinical director of SeaSide Palm Beach, an executive drug and alcohol rehabilitation program in Palm Beach, Florida, who has been working one-on-one with addicts and emotional eaters for more than twenty years. "We've been told that self-esteem grows as a function of your accomplishment. It seems perfectly obvious, but while an accomplishment does give you a feeling of pride, it's fleeting. If I have bad self-esteem, I could achieve until the cows come home and it won't make a dent in that. A lot of high-achieving people are really running from that sense of 'I'm not good enough.'"

That was certainly true for me. Deep down, I felt like dirt and

---

People have the power to grow, change, and heal.

---

was chasing ways to make myself feel better. Even when I did do well (which was more often than I allowed myself to believe), I would pooh-pooh it. When I'd get compliments, I'd shove them aside.

I still struggle at times with the feeling that because I'm not perfect I'm not entirely deserving of success, but it no longer gets in my way. By becoming aware of that tendency to discount my positive attributes and achievements, I've taken a lot of the power and sting out of it. When those thoughts pop into my head, I see them coming from miles away and I recognize them as the twisted, untrue beliefs that they are. First, I look at them and say, "Thanks for sharing, but I don't buy that anymore." Then I remind myself of the new truths I hold dear:

- I believe that each and every person on this earth is deserving of love, happiness, and success, simply because they exist. (That includes me!)

- I believe that people have the power to grow, change, and heal.

• I believe that—with obvious exceptions like violence, crime, and unethical behavior—nothing in this life is black or white. Nothing is purely good or evil, no person purely awful or angelic, no food intrinsically bad or good.

Do You Suffer from Black-and-White Thinking?

A couple of quick questions for you. Do you think that thin is good and fat is bad? Do you believe that there are "good" foods and "bad" foods? My guess is that you said yes and yes, just the way I would have a few years ago. Here's the thing: Those statements aren't true. They're both classic examples of black-and-white thinking, also called all-or-nothing or dichotomous thinking. Black-and-white thinking is a cognitive distortion—a term psychologists use to describe exaggerated or irrational thoughts that tend to cause distress. Cognitive distortions contribute to depression, anxiety, and eating disorders.

The first memory I have of black-and-white thinking in my own life happened when I was seven years old. It was Christmas Eve. My mother didn't feel well, so she stayed home, but she sent me, my older brother and sister, and my dad across the street to my grandparents' house for a big family dinner and gift opening. My grandma Rose was famous for her Christmas cookies—chocolate-butterscotch turtles, candy-cane twists, snickerdoodles—and as I've mentioned, in my house, I was famous for my appetite. Perhaps that's why, on my way out the door that holiday night, my mom said to me, "Don't eat too many cookies. Don't blow it!" She probably just didn't want me to overdose on sugar and get cranky, tired, and nauseated. But the message I heard was "Cookies are bad, and if you eat them, you are bad, too."

So what did I do that night? I ate thirteen cookies. I was keeping count because I wanted to be able to go home and tell my mom how "good" I'd been; but as the count increased, so did my shame—and there was no way I was going to tell her how many sweet things I ended up putting into my little tummy that night. I had been a bad girl. Even though my parents told me they loved me unconditionally—and I know they did—something inside me told me that good girls get love, bad girls are worthless. "Good" to me also came to mean thin and self-disciplined, and "bad" came to mean fat and out of control. This is a classic example of black-and-white thinking, one of the most common cognitive distortions that disordered eaters buy into, according to Dr. Bulik.

Thinking of foods as good or bad adds more than just guilt to eating certain things; it adds excitement, making the "bad" foods that you are trying so hard to avoid even more attractive. I don't know about you, but I'm much more likely to overdo it with something that's forbidden than with something I think of

---

There's no good or evil; there's just food.

---

as "good" or "healthy." In fact, just the guilt from putting one little taste of an evil food in my mouth used to be able to trigger a full-on binge.

"Although I am not nearly as severe as I was in the past, I do still have the black-and-white mentality when it comes to 'good' foods versus 'bad' foods," said Razieh. "It's still hard for me to view all foods the same. It's still difficult for me to enjoy a piece of chocolate and then continue the rest of my day not devouring three full chocolate bars. My eating disorder takes over and tells me 'Well, you ate one thing more than you should have, might as well eat everything in sight.' I am definitely on the track of improvement, but as everyone with an eating disorder knows, it is something that must be worked on every day."

But, you might ask, isn't it objectively true that some foods are just plain bad for you? There's no doubt that some items are more nutritious than others (more on this in Chapter 8), but here's how I try to look it now: There are some foods—mostly stuff that grows—that the body is ideally suited to using for fuel. Humans have been eating these things since we first stood up on two legs. And there are other foods that aren't meant as constant fuel, but as extras that we can use for fun, pleasure, and to make those main "fuel" foods taste better. There's no good or evil; there's just food. And as we get healthier in our thinking, we can decide what the best combinations of foods are for our bodies. It truly is different for everyone, and what's best for you when you're sixteen might not work very well for you when you're thirty.

By the way, black-and-white thinking is about way more than just food. No matter what part of our lives this mistaken belief system is applied to, it creates drama, guilt, and anxiety. My "If I'm not perfect, I suck" tendency is just another form of this irrational thought process. Some others?

- *Things didn't happen the way I thought they would this morning, so the whole day is ruined.*

- *If you're not the best, you're the worst.*

- *Believing something is "always" going to be the way it is right now and will "never" change.*

"The first thing to do is actually to become aware of your tendency to do this—not just around food but in all aspects of your life: Either I get an A or I fail; either my clothes are perfect or I look like a slob," said Dr. Bulik. "Once you identify all of the areas you tend to do this in, ask yourself some simple questions about it. Like, are there other alternatives? Are there possibilities in between these two extremes that might exist and are also likely outcomes? If it's about a test, what would the consequences be if I got a B? Is that *really* failing? How would someone who typically gets C's feel if they got a B—am I applying standards to myself that I would never apply to anyone else?"

---

exercise:
what irrational beliefs do you have?

There are dozens of cognitive distortions, but here are a few that Dr. Bulik said tend to be most common in emotional eaters. How many do you recognize? Put a check next to each that you identify with.

1. Black-and-white thinking: Thinking in "all-or-nothing" terms: *"I either have to lose fifty pounds or forget it,"* or *"I've already eaten two, I may as well eat twenty."*

2. Expecting perfection: Anything less than excellence means failure and it reflects upon your worth as a person. *"I have to lose two pounds a week or I am a failure."*

3. Magical thinking: You believe in strong links between unrelated events. *"If I lose twenty-five pounds, everything else will fall into place."*

4. Catastrophizing: Only paying attention to the negative side of things, or overestimating the chances of disaster. *"I sprained my ankle, I'm never going to be able to exercise again!"*

5. Personal ineffectiveness: Assuming you can do nothing to change your situation. *"Why should I even bother to tell her what she's doing hurts my feelings? She'll never listen to me anyhow."*

6. Overgeneralizing: Condemning yourself as a total person on the basis of a single event, or believing that if something turns out badly once, then it will always happen that way. *"I gained two pounds. I'm going to end up right back where I started."*

When you're feeling upset, bad about yourself, or like you're at risk of bingeing, it can help to sit down and ask yourself if you're employing any of these cognitive distortions. If so, what are some alternate stories you can tell yourself about what might happen? What would you say to a friend who was saying or thinking these things? What are some more kind, compassionate, and rational thoughts you can replace these distortions with?

How Traumatic Experiences in Our Pasts Push Us Toward Food

Research has shown that physical, sexual, and verbal abuse in childhood—whether it's perpetrated by adults, siblings or peers—is linked to binge eating and other disordered eating patterns like anorexia and bulimia. Many women I've met in binge eating support groups over the years have said they were abused when they were younger, and a few of the girls I interviewed for this book talked about it, too. "When I was very young, I was molested," said Jessica, thirty, who has dealt with restricting, bingeing, and purging. "In my mind, I felt that act was my fault and spent most of my life trying to please other people in order to make up for it. It made me feel that I was worth less than other people. And I always thought that if I were thinner, more athletic, etc., then people would like me more. I desperately wanted to be liked."

Kids who have been harmed in these ways can basically get emotionally stunted, said Drew Pinsky, M.D., who specializes in the treatment of addictions of all kinds and is the host of *Celebrity Rehab with Dr. Drew*. "Food is an emotional regulator. It helps you manage your feelings," he told me. "If you have childhood trauma, if you had terror in childhood, abandonment, neglect, abuse, you exit the process that builds your ability to learn regulation on your own. But you still have to regulate somehow." You haven't had the chance to learn healthy ways to do it, so what do you do? "We can cut, do drugs, and we can eat or have sex," said Dr. Drew. "These are primitive ways to regulate our feelings. To make ourselves feel okay. It's really a bid for survival, to help yourself feel like you can go on."

Anna, twenty-six, was sexually abused and believes that experience had a huge impact on her becoming a binge eater. "The truth is that for as much pain as the bingeing was causing, it was also numbing me to pain I had no idea how to deal with," she told me. "When I was five I was sexually abused. Episodes of abuse continued until I was nine years old. Those awful experiences left me full of secrets, shame, and emotions I was too young to make any sense of. I thought maybe the abuse was something I caused or invited, so I kept it all to myself. Without guidance or support, the effects of the abuse were mine to carry alone, and it was exhausting. Bingeing kept the secrets I carried stuffed under huge amounts of food. It also kept my body safe under a layer of fat that I was certain rendered me completely gross and unattractive to boys."

The feeling that fat can protect you is an extremely common

Food is an emotional regulator.
It helps you manage your feelings.

---

one among emotional overeaters. "Many women actually over-eat to desexualize themselves, take themselves out of the target zone of a male predator," said Dr. Lukens. "The fat is a protection, a buffer. They're using their size on purpose in a sense." In fact, there is a classic syndrome among women who have been significantly obese and then get Lap-Band or other weight-loss surgeries: "They lose a bunch of weight, they lose that protective barrier or that big body around them, and they freak out," said Dr. Drew. "So many end up with depression. They've lost their primary defense. It's very common. It happens to men, too."

I wasn't sexually abused or violated as a child. But when I was in my teens, a guy I dated coerced me into a sexual act that I didn't want to happen. Even worse, he didn't listen when I verbally asked him to stop, and didn't stop even after I began to cry. I didn't call it rape at the time, but I knew what happened wasn't okay, and I broke up with him the next day. As I got older, after having some therapy, I realized that what he'd done was a grave violation—of my body and my trust. We were dating at the time, we'd both been drinking, and as I said, it was more a case of coercion than physcial force. But in at least one sense, what he did was clearly illegal: He was over twenty and I was under eighteen. In California, that meant he had committed statutory rape. I told my mother about it, and we talked about the possibility of pressing charges, but I decided I didn't want to—I was scared to talk about it in court, I was scared of what he'd say to the police and lawyers, and I wanted to move on. (I don't have many regrets in life, but not allowing my parents to prosecute him is one of them.) In my early twenties, I became increasingly uncomfortable with the looks I would sometimes get from men. Even if they weren't obviously leering, just having their eyes on me, on my body, made me want to jump out of my skin. It made me feel unsafe and angry. I can't help wondering if one reason I ended up weighing 225 pounds was that I wanted to protect myself from ever being hurt sexually again.

That violation didn't cause my emotional eating, of course. I believe I was genetically predisposed to this, and that it was the trauma of my parents' divorce that really kicked my binge eating disorder into gear. That fact used to make me feel weak. My parents got divorced, so what? It happens to lots of kids, and they don't all run out and get eating disorders! Families splitting up may be commonplace, but research shows that divorce is actually incredibly traumatic for everyone involved. The children often feel abandoned and shaken. I know I did. It was like the fabric of my whole life was dissolving. I remember having a dream during that time that I was standing between my mother and father, up in the sky on a puffy cloud. The cloud started breaking up and drifting apart under my feet, and as each of their halves floated away, I fell.

In addition to the general disruption, sadness, and anger that divorce can inject into a kid's life, the children often tend to be alone more—and loneliness is a big trigger for emotional eating.

"My parents split up when I was ten," said Rachael. "My brother and I would often come home from school and have to make food for ourselves. We lived in a tiny house without a dining table, so we never ate dinner as a family. My brother would often comment on the large portions I would eat. I had started eating heaps after school because I was bored and lonely and then putting myself to bed early to sleep it off and because I was too full and sad to do anything else."

It's not just capital-T Trauma like abuse or divorce that can knock a person off-kilter and plunge them into disordered eating. Pain can come in much subtler packages. "There's an awful lot of trauma in people's lives," Rebecca Radcliffe told me. "We tend to think about physical and sexual abuse. We think of trauma as overpowering, big, loud, boisterous, there's a rape, a beating. But there is also neglect, or low-grade remarks that are made, a disinterest from parents, and when you add it up day after day, year after year, those things undermine a person's sense of self. A child can be made to think, 'Who will care for me? Am I in the world by myself?' It might not look 'traumatic' from the outside, but there's a lot of pain."

Sarah told me she felt alone in the world as a child. "I was lonely because I was really shy and not that sociable," she said. "I tried to make friends but the majority of the people around me were older than I was. When I was eating, I didn't feel so alone. I remember this one time when I was eleven where I bought six individual-size bags of chips and ate them in one sitting. I think that incident was the first time I ate so much because I was feeling lonely." Of course, tendencies toward disordered eating just served to make Sarah feel even more different from and rejected by those around her. "When I was in middle school, I noticed that everyone did not eat as much as I did, and I knew that what I was doing was not healthy," she said. "I was ashamed of it, and I still am."

This sense of being "different" from other people came up a lot with the young women I interviewed for this book. Like Trish: "I remember in the fifth grade, my school sold milk at lunch—skim, whole, and chocolate—and all my friends would always get skim milk. I would drink two chocolate-milk boxes while my friends were satisfied with only one of the skim milk," she told me. "I not only didn't eat or drink like the other girls, but I was gaining height and weight. I was a C-cup in fifth grade, so I didn't look like the other girls, either. I had braces, I hadn't grown into my nose yet, I had terrible acne, and I had huge boobs. Boys and girls alike would talk about me behind my back. The awful nicknames kids can come up with are ridiculous. By seventh grade the boys were referring to me as 'Patitsa' instead of 'Patricia'; the boys would stare at me during gym class and the girls would just get jealous and spread rumors about me."

One study by Dianne Neumark-Sztainer, Ph.D., at the University of Minnesota, found that 63 percent of overweight teen girls had experienced some kind of teasing about their weight—as had 48 percent of underweight girls and 21 percent of average-weight girls. That kind of teasing can be really harmful and even push some people into eating disorders who might not have developed them otherwise, said Dr. Sophy. "We always say words and names can't hurt you, but they can," he explains. "Being told by someone, whether it's your peers or parents, that you're fat or weak or somehow unacceptable in some way can really get into your head and make you think that about yourself, too. As kids, you believe that's what and who you are."

"I have come to think there are very few people who get through life unscathed from one type of trouble or another," Radcliffe told me. "I remember watching my father pay the bills and he'd be yelling. We'd go hide in the closet! When I reflect back, I think that was traumatic. Whether it was watching parents fighting or cheating or having to move or having family financial troubles or illness," there are a lot of difficult and painful events that can leave you shaken, vulnerable, and scared. Dr. Lukens agrees: "Every child is overwhelmed at some point and that feeling is categorized as 'stuff to be avoided.' That's what drives the need for the self-medicating with food." We're using the food to avoid feeling things that make us uncom-

---

We're using the food to avoid feeling things that make us uncomfortable.

---

fortable. We often don't even know what those specific feelings are. As soon as a whiff of some difficult or scary emotion—abandonment, loneliness, rejection, fear of violation—bubbles up, our binge response kicks in. "Guilt, shame, anger, sadness, you feel them encroaching on your awareness and it's anxiety-provoking," said Dr. Lukens. "You get triggered and you go into a trance and engage in your avoidance strategy, which is eating. You don't even want to know what it is that you're avoiding." Said Kendra: "If I feel stressed, lonely, mad, or sad at all, I automatically think of something I can eat that will ease that pain, but I don't think about it when I'm actually bingeing. When I binge or overeat, it feels as though my brain shuts off."

Bringing some awareness to the reasons why we're feeling the urge to eat emotionally—especially in the moments before we take that first bite—can be extremely helpful in interrupting the binge cycle. "Ask yourself, 'What am I avoiding? I must be avoiding something if this impulse is triggered,'" said Dr. Lukens.

exercise:
what are you avoiding?

The next time you feel the urge to binge, ask yourself, "What am I avoiding?" Don't allow yourself to slip into that food trance before settling on at least one possibility. Then, even if you do end up eating emotionally or bingeing, at least you made a connection in your mind and began a new practice. The next time, you may be able to dig a little deeper, find out more about yourself, and eventually even avoid a binge.

Overeating was a good coping mechanism for you at first. It may have protected you from danger or, like a drug, soothed pain you didn't have any other way to deal with. It may have helped you avoid looking at emotions that you didn't have the tools to deal with. But I'm willing to guess that avoiding these feelings isn't working so well for you anymore. As you get healthier and more aware, you'll gain the strength to face them. You'll learn to use new tools to deal with them, and you'll be able to reach out for more help if you need it.

Your Turn:

1. Do you believe you may have low self-esteem? If so, where do you think it stems from? Perfectionism? Other people's expectations? Traumatic experiences as a child? Other sources of shame?

2. If, as Dr. Lukens said, achievement doesn't help boost self-esteem, what types of things could you do to make your-

self feel stronger and more worthwhile? Could taking care of yourself emotionally—doing things like reading this book, for example, or expressing your opinions and desires to friends and family—make you feel better about yourself?

3. Have you ever used binge eating to "take yourself out of the game," as Morgan described? What things have you avoided doing, trying, or being because of your eating and body issues, and why?

4. Did you experience trauma as a child, teen, or even as an adult? Looking back, what connections can you draw between that trauma and your current issues with emotional overeating?

chapter five

Yes, You *Can* Interrupt a Binge

At some point in our lives, bingeing has helped us. We emotional overeaters developed this behavior as a way to protect ourselves and deal with feelings and events that we didn't have tools to cope with. As human animals, our number one goal is to survive—and overeating has, no doubt, been a survival tool for us. Just think about all the things it has meant to you over the years: comfort, relaxation, distraction, company, an outlet for anger and anxiety, a break from your busy life and even a dose of mood-improving brain chemicals when you were down. Of course, food was never meant to do and be all of these things. It's most basic, true purpose is to be fuel for our bodies. So, how did it become our go-to tool for all of these other needs?

It really isn't about the food at all.
It's more about emotions and feelings that
are hard to deal with or have been pushed
away in the past, and the overeating is just a
coping mechanism to deal with those
emotions and numb them.

Remember when I told you about the time I ate all those fund-raising candy bars in high school? Well, when that happened, I knew something was terribly wrong with my relationship with food—and after I had to ask my mom for the money to pay for them, so did she. That's when she sent me to see Mitch, the family therapist my parents had been seeing throughout their separation. Mitch taught me something I will never forget. He said that what I was doing with food was "impulse substitution." When someone is sad, for example, their impulse may be to cry; if they're angry, their impulse may be to yell. But food had become my go-to way to deal with almost any need. So when I was sad, instead of having the urge to cry, I'd have the urge to eat. When I was angry, instead of having the urge to express it, my impulse was to eat. Mitch told me that, although eating had become my default, I could start to retrain myself to use other, more appropriate and much more effective tools instead of food. He encouraged me to do three things whenever I had the urge to eat when I wasn't hungry:

- pause

- try to name the emotion or need that I had

- think of other possible ways to soothe or fill it

We're going to do Mitch's exercise for a few of the binge triggers we talk about in this chapter. But first, let's talk about the things that drive us to eat, what food does for us, and what we can try to do instead. Hillary, twenty-four, told me: "The biggest thing I've learned is that it really isn't about the food at all. It's more about emotions and feelings that are hard to deal with or had been pushed away in the past, and the overeating is just a coping mechanism to deal with those emotions and numb them."

Trigger: Stress Overload

I asked every young woman I interviewed for this book what feelings and circumstances seemed to trigger her binges. The answer I heard most often? "Stress!" We're all pretty stressed these days: A national survey by the American Psychological

Association found that 28 percent of women reported having an average stress level of eight, nine, or ten on a ten-point scale. Forty-nine percent of women in this same survey said they had eaten too much or eaten "unhealthy" foods because of stress in the last month. Believe me, I get it. Every month at work, when the latest issue of the magazine I work for goes to print, the whole staff has a few days that are incredibly busy. I'm often working on several stories for each issue, and during these few super-pressure-filled days I'm doing about a hundred things at once: trimming words so that the stories fit into the page layouts; working with researchers in the fact-checking department to make sure that every single fact, statistic, and quote is accurate; and writing and rewriting headlines and captions. Adding to the pressure, everything we do during that part of the process has an effect on everyone else on staff. A delay of a couple of hours on my end can mean that someone in another department may have to stay late to work on the page that night. (My heart's beating a little faster just thinking about it!)

Truth be told, it's incredibly exciting work, and the deadline pressure is one reason why I wanted to become a journalist in the first place. When I give in to it and just go with the flow—focusing on one task after another, knowing that this is how it is for today and even enjoying the ride—I'm fine. But when I find myself pushing or struggling against it, thinking about how "stressed" I am and how much I have to do, indulging in thoughts like, *I'll never be able to get it all done* or dwelling on how "crazy" things are, I start to feel panicky, overwhelmed, and sometimes even resentful. That's when you're in danger of your thoughts turning to food. What can I eat to make this day better? I'm working so hard that I deserve something extra yummy. Mac 'n cheese, perhaps? A big, bready sandwich with bacon and lots of mayo? Potato chips? It's perfectly okay for me to eat any and all of those things, but the idea that any of those foods can actually fix anything other than physical hunger is what can be dangerous for emotional eaters. "I work full-time for a great nonprofit organization in Boston where I assist people in need with emergency food resources like food pantries, soup kitchens, and food stamps," Razieh told me. "It's an extremely rewarding job, but like any job, can be very stressful at times. When I get frustrated with a stressful caller, my immediate thought is to binge. I can fight it pretty well when I stop and recognize it, but there are, of course, the times where it seems uncontrollable."

Here's the thing about "stress," though: I think we've all learned to use that word too loosely. We use it as a blanket term to cover a whole range of emotions that may actually require very different techniques and tools to deal with. We say "I'm so stressed!" when what we really mean is something like "I'm feeling overwhelmed by tasks at work," "I'm angry at the way my family is acting," "I'm scared that I won't be able to pay my credit card this month"—or a combination of a bunch of things like that. I've found that the first step in avoiding a binge and finding a healthier way to deal with feeling "stressed out" is to drill down to a more specific description of what's going on. Take Razieh, for instance. When she talked earlier about her "stressful caller," I wondered if what she was really feeling was frustration. Anyone who's worked a customer-service, retail, or phone-based job can tell you that dealing with members of the public can be incredibly frustrating. When I say I'm stressed at work, perhaps what I'm feeling is more specifically being overwhelmed by the sheer volume of what needs to get done. We both used the word *stressed* to describe what we were feeling, but frustration is very different from being overwhelmed—and the two emotions require completely different ways of coping. When I stop to think about it, I realize that when I'm frustrated, I need to blow off steam. To do something big and loud. Maybe close my office door and swear and throw a few papers around. Post a quick and bitchy update on Facebook about how much I hate whatever just happened. Instant-message my husband, John, or text my best friend, Cheri, and just completely go off. But when I'm overwhelmed? I usually just need to cry or take a walk. Once I do that, I can get into solution mode; then, with a clear mind, I look at what's on my to-do list and decide what to tackle first and what will simply have to wait.

exercise:
impulse substitution

The next time you find yourself feeling stressed and thinking of turning to food, pause for a moment and ask yourself what you're really feeling. Are you frustrated? Overwhelmed? Answer the following questions on a piece of paper or in a journal:

1. What are you feeling?

2. What do you need?

3. What would eating in this situation give you?

4. What can you do instead?

Here's how Razieh might have filled out this exercise:

1. What are you feeling? *Frustrated!!*

2. What do you need? *To blow off some steam.*

3. What would eating in this situation give you? *A release of pent-up energy.*

4. What can you do instead? *Call someone I trust and just vent.*

Here's how I might fill it out next time a deadline approaches:

1. What are you feeling? *Overwhelmed, like I'll never finish all of this work.*

2. What do you need? *Something to clear my head.*

3. What would eating in this situation give you? *A momentary break, but it would end up making my brain even fuzzier.*

4. What strategy can you use instead? *Cry! Then I can go back to my work with a sharper mind.*

Trigger: Anger

I also believe we sometimes say we're stressed when what we really mean is we're angry. Anger is a tough emotion for many women to deal with, said Dr. Bulik. "It seems easier for us to talk about the role of depression and anxiety in binge eating and less so about anger, yet stuffing down anger is something I hear so often from patients," she said. "We all have faced 'rules' about appropriate ways for women to express anger. Sometimes it is not okay at all. When we do get appropriately angry, sometimes it freaks people out, or they find it unfitting, off-putting, scary even. When a man boss gets angry, things happen! When a woman boss gets angry, she has PMS. Plus some women are simply scared to express anger. It is a powerful emotion that can lead them to fear being rejected, precisely because they expressed their anger. This fear can be enough to prompt them to put the brakes on the emotion and stuff it down with food instead."

Kate, twenty-nine, said the idea that anger could trigger a binge didn't click for her until she read a passage from a book by Ben Sonder called *Eating Disorders: When Food Turns Against You* that she'd checked out from the library. "In the description of angry eating, Sonder said that if a child, while learning to assert themselves, meets with a harsh reaction from parents, that part of development is stunted," she explained. "Or if a child spends a lot of time with an angry or violent family member, anger is seen as an emotional state to be avoided, and the child tries to be nice, agreeable, and pleasant. I've been thinking about this a lot. I'm not assertive at all. It's now such a habit, being this nice, agreeable Kate."

Oftentimes, on some deeper level, women are afraid that showing their anger is going to wreck a relationship. "There's so much destructive anger out there and not much positive use of it," said Rebecca Radcliffe. "But we need to recognize that we do get angry about things. We all have this emotion, and we can have it quite frequently." So how do we appropriately process and deal with this scary feeling without turning to food or striking out so roughly that we hurt a relationship with someone we love? For me, it's incredibly important not to let anger or resentment build up and fester. If I allow either one of those emotions to stick around for too long, it sort of thickens into this icky emotional gunk that starts to affect the way I deal with people and situations that are totally unrelated to what was bothering me in the first place. Letting these "injuries" pile up without dealing with the feelings and confronting the situation is like putting myself in an emotional pressure cooker; when that thing finally explodes, look out!

"We need role models and practice with being angry," said Dr. Bulik. "Even just learning how to say 'that makes me angry or disappointed' is a first step. Someone who works with me told a wonderful story about a day when she was just steamed— all she wanted to do was vent. Her husband was all about trying to get her to calm down, to relax, not to take things so seriously. She got even more angry and just said, 'I will calm down when it is time to calm down, it is now time to be angry, and I have every intention of staying angry until I am completely ready not to be angry anymore!'"

We all feel anger. But if you don't know how—or think you're not allowed—to express it, you might just tear into a sandwich or fiercely finish off a bag of chips instead. I know I used to. Years ago, a mentor in my binge eating support group suggested that I start something she called a "God Box." There's nothing inherently religious about it—and you can use it whether you believe in "God" or not. The basic idea is that you write down any issues, worries, or problems you've been having on a slip of paper, then fold it up and put it in a special box that you use only for that purpose. It's a physical, tangible way of saying to yourself and the universe that you want to let this problem or worry go. Whenever I put something in my God Box, I tell myself something like: "I'm not in control of everything and that's okay. I give up obsessing about this thing and trust that God/the universe/my intuition/my healthy inner self will take care of me."

The God Box worked wonders for me, and helped me let go of a lot of worries over the years. So when I noticed recently that I was getting irritated and angry at work more than usual, I created an "Angry Box"! I know that I can't let these thoughts stick around in the air and fester so anytime I find myself bugged when I'm at the office and it's not a situation that requires me to speak up or stand up for myself, I simply write my thoughts down on a Post-it note, fold it up, and put it in the box. Out of my head and into the box it goes. Whew!

Trigger: Anxiety!!!

Anxiety—that awful pitlike feeling in your stomach that's just screaming to be filled with food. "For the longest time I would work out intensely and restrict my eating after binge episodes instead of looking it in the eye and trying to understand it," said Razieh. "I have noticed a pattern with my binges. Feeling even the slightest bit anxious about something triggers me. It can be something as minor as being nervous about going to a holiday party, or a work deadline, or a money situation." Anxiety was a big one for me, too. Through my midtwenties, it was often at its worst on Sunday afternoons and evenings. I remember talking to my therapist (more about therapy in Chapter 6) about it: I wanted to binge nearly every Sunday night, and we figured out that it was because I was worrying about work the next day; what would happen, what I'd have to do, if I'd mess something up, sometimes even just the fact that I had to put makeup on, make myself presentable, and be around people.

The thought of being around people used to make Casey, a twenty-two-year-old who is recovering from binge eating disorder, anxious, too. "I wish I was a carefree, fly-by-the-seat-of-my-pants kind of person, but I'm just not that girl," she told me. "I'm a worrier by nature, always have been, but my insecurities hit an all-time high when I came to college. I didn't know how to deal with all of the what-ifs on my own, and I quickly discovered that overeating was a great distraction. It obviously didn't take care of my worries, but my little 'cookie comas' turned out to be quite an effective way to numb my mind. I started seeing a therapist on campus, not just for my eating issues, but also for some pretty deep-rooted anxiety problems. It turns out, I have social anxiety and probably have for years. This helps explain a lot of the things I did that I never understood, like coming home from dinner with friends only to eat a few packages of Oreos or recovering from a class presentation with a box of Pop-Tarts."

Razieh also sees the connection between anxiety and her eating. "Loneliness, rejection, feeling overwhelmed with deadlines, and watching my bank account decline are all triggers for my bingeing," she told me. "I've also noticed that I want to eat when I don't have a plan, like coming home after work and not having plans for the gym or plans with friends or even 'laundry-night' plans. But being around others and doing things I like—baths, calling a friend, painting my nails—lessen these thoughts about bingeing."

Another thing that used to make me anxious—and still does, at times—is unstructured time. Want to see Sunny squirm? Just give me a day off with no plans and nothing to "be done." When my husband and I were just friends, before we started dating, he used to tease me about having such a packed social calendar. We'd often have to wait two or three weeks before meeting up for dinner or drinks because I had so many other things planned. It's not because I was so darn popular; it's because I literally couldn't allow myself any time off. Free time for me equaled major anxiety and set me up for a binge. I think Rebecca Radcliffe described it perfectly in her book *Enlightened Eating*: The "empty hours stretching on ahead" make us feel empty, and we often just want to find ways to make time pass. One way is to eat. "Every minute drags by reminding us of how alone we are," she writes. In my case, I think there might be some fear involved, too—specifically fear of being lazy and of not accomplishing enough.

I know now that this fear probably goes back to my old self-esteem issues and perfectionistic tendencies. But sometimes I still find myself feeling uncomfortable when an afternoon stretches out in front of me and I don't have anything on tap. So what do I do? I'll often ask myself if I really actually *want* to do anything. If the answer is yes, I find something to do—rearrange my closet, do the dishes, meet a friend for lunch. If the answer is no, I make a "plan" to do nothing. I tell myself that my only to-do for this whole block of time is . . . nothing. If I feel like watching TV for five hours, I'm allowed to watch TV for five hours, because that was the plan! (Let me tell you, if you've never done nothing for an entire day 100 percent guilt-free, you should try it. It's truly fabulous.)

Anxiety is still the most difficult emotion for me to manage. I used food as an antianxiety drug for almost fifteen years. But now I know that I have a choice in the matter. Sure, I could try to escape anxiety with food, but that never works for long. So most times, I choose to face it—starting with thinking or writing about what the real cause of my anxiety might be. Sometimes it takes longer than others to figure out, but it's always something. Then, if there is an action I can take that will resolve the cause of the anxiety, I take that action. Say it's a Sunday night and I'm anxious about work the next day. I'll log on to my calendar to see what's on deck so I feel more mentally prepared; or I'll text myself a little to-do list of things I need to remember. If I'm anxious because an unfinished task like replying to e-mails or paying bills is nagging at the back of my brain, I tackle the task or schedule a time to do it. If I truly don't know what I'm anxious about, I talk to someone about it. Often just putting it out in the open and out of my head brings a little relief.

More Binge Triggers: Do Any of These Make You Want to Overeat?

Stress, anger, and anxiety aren't the only things that can lead to binges (not by a long shot). Here's a list of other triggers I've noticed in my own life and that girls I've interviewed for this book have mentioned. Do you tend to overeat because of any of these things? If so, pause and ask yourself: The next time I'm in this situation or feel this way, what can I do to get what I need rather than eat?

Being rejected by a guy
Being drunk or tipsy
Feeling happy or excited
Being bored
Feeling lonely
Simply being alone in the house or apartment
Watching TV
Feeling like you need a break
Sadness
The sun going down (night eating)   ✳

A Very Real, Very Serious Binge Trigger: Depression

I went through my first bout of depression in my late teens. You'll remember that my parents divorced when I was fifteen, and it shook me up pretty badly. Well, I graduated from high school just two years later, and I still wasn't in such great shape. I didn't feel ready to move on to college—and all I did for a few months was lie on the couch, watch TV, and eat. I felt hopeless, sad and scared, and didn't enjoy anything anymore except for chewing and swallowing.

Not every binge eater has depression, but several studies have found a strong link between the two. One found that overweight women who binge ate were three times as likely to have depression than overweight women who didn't binge. So, does the bingeing cause the depression or do we binge because we're depressed? No one has sorted that out just yet, but I'd bet that it's a little of both. The fact is, eating large amounts of food—especially sugary, fatty, or carbohydrate-heavy food—causes your brain to produce more of the feel-good chemical serotonin. The food becomes almost like a natural tranquilizer or antidepressant. Obviously, self-medicating a serious mood disorder that way creates more problems than it solves, and food never gives anything more than very temporary relief.

With time and continued occasional counseling sessions

with our family therapist, Mitch, I was able to get up off the couch and—still just eighteen years old—I got a part-time job as a bank teller and enrolled in classes at a local community college. I was functioning, but I still wasn't feeling right. I cried a lot and felt generally sad much of the time. One semester, I had to drop all my classes because I had such difficulties getting myself motivated and out of the house. By age twenty, after one particularly wrenching sobbing session, my new boyfriend (he's the one whom I was briefly married to in college) pointed out that the way I was feeling and acting wasn't normal and might be depression. I went to my doctor. He diagnosed me with mild depression and gave me a prescription for an antidepressant. The medication didn't cure my binge eating, but it lifted the intense sadness. I started being able to think more clearly and felt like I could handle being out in life again, despite my continuing to binge a couple times a week. If I hadn't been treated for the underlying depression, I don't think I would've been able to start focusing on healing my disordered eating.

Strategies for Avoiding a Binge and Getting What You Really Need

Handling a tough feeling—whether it's anger, resentment, frustration, sadness, loneliness, betrayal, humiliation, or anything else—is a two-step process, according to Radcliffe. First we need something immediate that we can pull out of our pocket to relieve some of the intensity of the feeling. (This is what Radcliffe and other psychological experts often call "discharging" an emotion.) Then, once we're calmer, we can think about what triggered that emotion and what a constructive way to deal with that problem or situation might be. We've already started to come up with some of these instant strategies with the impulse substitution exercises earlier in this chapter, but you'll likely need a lot more.

In fact, Radcliffe recommends that every one of us make a list of twenty-five things we can do when different feelings arise. "If a person's default to deal with stress is grabbing a Snickers or eating a brownie, I don't think the default thing is necessarily bad," she told me. "But if eating a brownie is the only thing they have to rely on, then they are going to need twenty-five brownies to do the trick. I often tell people that they may need two or three or four of their strategies to deal with one event. Take a walk, then call a friend, then do something else. It takes the burden off the food." It's important to have so many different options, she said, because you'll be sure to have one that applies and will help no matter what your situation. "I don't think that the same calming method works for all of our emotions," she said. "What we're feeling when we're betrayed and what we need to do to handle that feeling is very different than if someone special just died and we're grieving and at a loss. If we're overwhelmed, or if we're confused, we'll also need something different." (In a fabulous little book she wrote called *Dance Naked in Your Living Room*, Radcliffe came up with 120 activities to suit every emotion.)

Here are the strategies I have on my own list, and the emotions they tend to be helpful for. As you read through these, ask yourself if you think any would work for you. If so, star them or grab a notebook and jot them down. Then make a complete list of your own.

1. Reading an energizing or inspiring book (tired, sad, generally blue)

2. Going for a quick jog (anxious, angry, nervous, sluggish, overworked)

3. Writing a blog post (happy, excited, sad)

4. Talking to my husband, John, about whatever's going on (works for pretty much all emotions)

5. Venting on Facebook (frustrated, angry, happy, excited)

6. Putting stuff in my God Box or Angry Box (worried, anxious, nervous, scared, mad, resentful)

7. Doing the dishes or cleaning up the house (worried, anxious, bored, confused, scattered)

8. Journaling (works for any emotion)

9. Going out for a cup of coffee (bored, overwhelmed, tired)

10. Simply getting up from where I am and going into another room to do something else (bored, tired)

11. Making a list (anxious, overwhelmed)

12. Walking around outside (bored, anxious, happy)

13. Making plans to do something with a friend in the future (lonely, bored, happy, excited)

14. Texting a friend (lonely, bored)

15. Listening to a guided meditation (works for lots of emotions—more on meditation in the next chapter)

16. Having a small glass of wine or a beer (tired, happy)

17. Cooking dinner from scratch (bored, uneasy, confused, scattered)

18. Reading fun blogs (bored, tired, overworked)

19. Taking a Pilates class (tired, overworked, body image distress)

20. Calling my mom (sad, happy, excited, needy, vulnerable)

21. Making a phone date with good friends who live out of town (lonely, excited)

22. Deep-breathing for five or ten minutes (overwhelmed, angry, sad)

23. Doing my nails (bored, confused, scattered, overworked)

24. Taking a bath or shower (sad, sluggish, tired)

25. Having a good cry (overwhelmed, sad, angry)

You might be surprised to see "crying" on my list. Just take a second to think about the phrase *having a good cry*—now think about the last time you had one. Didn't a part of you feel clearer, cleaner, and perhaps even refreshed afterward? Crying can be an incredibly powerful way to start to process certain emotions.

"I think it's like a rainstorm," said Radcliffe. "Things build up, the air gets thick, there's unease in the atmosphere, and then it rains. Sometimes the rainstorms are quiet and easy and gentle, but other times they're loud and awful. But afterward, the air is cleared, it's cleaner and sweeter. I think that happens with crying, too. The junk gets cleared away."

Over the years, I've found crying to be an incredibly important release for everything from true sadness and grief to simply feeling tired or overwhelmed. "There's an awful lot of sadness and confusion and worry, there's a lot of different emotions that need to be released," said Radcliffe. "Frequently our emotions are so uncomfortable that we're trying to cover them up by eat-

---

Frequently our emotions are so uncomfortable that we're trying to cover them up by eating. But if we are trying to learn to get beyond that process, we have to learn to feel those feelings and release them.

---

ing. But if we are trying to learn to get beyond that process, we have to learn to feel those feelings and release them. When we're uncomfortable and bothered and off balance, we're in a position of stress, and our bodies need to release that or it gets toxic and kills us. Crying discharges the emotion. Afterward we feel better—and then we don't have to work so hard to stuff those feelings all back inside."

Is crying going to solve your problems? No. But it can help you connect with the pain of, say, your boss or someone you're dating being disrespectful to you, instead of avoiding the pain by overeating. Then, once you get in touch with the way that job or relationship makes you feel, you can actually start to think about how to change or heal it!

Crying isn't easy for everyone. Some of us were taught as kids that crying was irritating or weak and that we shouldn't be "crybabies" about stuff. For me, it reminds me of when I was depressed and I cried much, much too often. So, even though crying was totally allowed in my family and even though I have experienced how cleansing and helpful a good cry can be, I sometimes still have a hard time letting myself go there. During one of our interviews, I told Radcliffe that when I'm especially busy, I feel as if I simply don't have time to cry—that I need to just suck it up, keep my head down, and plow through until I have less to do. "The thing that people might get afraid of is that if the grief or sorrow or worry is so heavy, if that chasm is so deep, they may start crying and never stop," she told me. "It's easier to stay in the rough-and-tumble levels of life where we're just trying to get through it and be efficient than to go into that really tender and vulnerable place." What she said, of course, made me want to cry. Instead of stuffing it down with food or work or anything else, when we got off the phone, I let the tears come. After a few minutes of just letting the deep sobs sweep over me, I tapped into the real emotion behind it. See, Radcliffe had given me a nice compliment during our talk about what I was doing with this book, and two of my core issues—perfectionism and low self-esteem—made that hard for me to take. It's kinda crazy the stuff that comes up when we no longer stuff it down with chocolate chip cookies.

Morgan has her own method for trying to derail a binge: "A helpful thing that my mom used to say when you start feeling the urge to reach for food or binge is to practice saying to yourself: 'HALT!' Actually stop, and check in to see if you are H—

hungry; A—angry or anxious; L—lonely; or T—tired. I find that when I get weird with food and overeat, these situations or feelings are often the triggers. Being aware of 'HALT' as triggers for me helps me catch myself and use nonfood ways to get what I need."

Another strategy that's been key for me is journaling and writing. The truth is, sometimes we don't have any idea what we're feeling—we just know that we feel like we really want to stuff food into our mouths. Writing has often helped me figure it out. "Journaling discharges emotion in a safe, private space, and it doesn't have to be edited," said Radcliffe. "You can hit the page with your pen, you can do whatever you want, no one's grading it. You can say nasty, mean things; it doesn't matter. I love it for that." Morgan said writing also helps her handle tough emotions without turning to food. "Writing in my journal—a sort of free-form stream-of-consciousness whatever-comes-to-mind—gets some of that energy out that might have gone into a binge," she explains. What's more, journaling and writing about our feelings or situation can also help us tap into our intuition and come up with solutions. "When we get the junk out, when we can release the negativity and confusion and hurt and pain, what can surface are deeper thoughts for who we are and what we want," said Radcliffe. "Who am I, what do I want, what do I need, and how do I get there?"

Remember: There's no "right" way to journal (or to do any of this stuff, for that matter). Whether you write a little every night to sort of digest your day and see what comes up, or in the mornings to center your thoughts, or just once in a while to help you figure out why you want to binge, it's all good.

As I bring this chapter to a close, I want to share a question with you that I've asked myself many, many times over the years. This single question has probably helped my recovery along more than just about anything else I've ever read, heard, or learned: What am I getting out of overeating? What is it about bingeing that is actually *benefiting* me? It may appear as if the relationship we have with our weird food behavior is pure hate and that if we could, we'd never overeat again starting right this very instant. But the truth is that if you're still emotionally overeating, still bingeing and restricting, still obsessing over food and your body, you're still getting something out of it. If you want to start to let food go, you'll need other strategies and coping mechanisms to put in its place.

Your Turn:

1. Does feeling "stressed" ever make you want to eat? Think of the last time you were stressed out and try to drill down to a deeper, more specific emotion you might have been feeling: Were you feeling overwhelmed? Overworked? Angry?

2. Make a list of at least five emotions or situations that you believe may trigger your binges. Next to each one, write a

strategy you could use instead of food to soothe, relieve, or help you deal with that emotion.

3. You are not a failure if you still choose food over other strategies—it may take a while to build up the strength to change. But are you ready to try to substitute healthier coping strategies for bingeing? If you're not ready yet, what can you do to get yourself there?

chapter six

The Emotional "Toolbox" Every Young Woman Needs

Before I recovered from binge eating, I was a somewhat inconsistent person. It was difficult for me to stick with things. I was always and forever running late. I was generally unorganized, scattered, and forgetful. In high school, my bedroom was so messy and there were so many clothes piled up on the floor that you could barely open the door. I procrastinated constantly. In college, I was always late for classes. After college, I was often late for work. I couldn't keep my schedule straight and would miss doctors' and sometimes even business appointments. When I started one-on-one psychotherapy when I was about twenty-six, I was even late to counseling sessions or would forget altogether. My therapist started sending me reminder e-mails the day before so I would be sure to show up. My credit-card and student-loan payments—even my rent—were frequently paid weeks late.

Today, my friends no longer have to wait ten, fifteen, twenty minutes for me when I tell them I'll meet them somewhere. The thought that my therapist (whom I still see every few weeks) would have to send me a reminder about an appointment is laughable. I'm actually known for meeting my deadlines at work. I'm juggling a full-time job, running HealthyGirl.org, and writing this book all at the same time. Oh, and of course, I no longer actively binge! How did all this happen? It's no mystery and it's certainly not magic: It's because of what I like to call my "toolbox."

This toolbox has helped me build self-esteem, it's helped calm my mind, it's helped me feel my feelings, it's helped me get to a healthier weight, it's helped me become more consistent and reliable, it's helped me succeed in my career, it's helped me find the man I married, it's helped me stop emotionally eating, it's helped me change. What's in it? Two different types of tools: instant ones, like the strategies we talked about in the last chapter, that help me deal with emotions and events in the moment; and ongoing, long-term tools that help me stay clearheaded and sane. It's the ongoing ones that I want to share with you now. Different ongoing tools will work better for different people, and will work better at different times in our lives. I've used every single one of these tools at various times in my life—and still use them regularly. Are you ready to mix and match and build your own toolbox? Here's some info you can use to get started.

Tool: Physical Activity

My mom absolutely loved to work out. She did jazzercise, weight training, Jane Fonda videos, Rollerblading—the woman taught aerobics when she was pregnant with me. So, it's perhaps no surprise that I felt exactly the opposite way growing up. I hated exercise. There's a picture of me at about age twelve in a hot-pink leotard; my hair's up in a clip, and I'm doing one of my mom's workout videos. I looked miserable, and I was. I think that was the only time I did that workout, and I managed to escape more sweating until the age of fourteen, when my mom wanted me to lose a couple pounds before homecoming. Suffice it to say that despite my mother's healthy love of exercising, I came to believe working out was a punishment for having an imperfect body. It was something a woman had to do in order to burn calories and correct the ugly, flabby mistakes in her form. Outside of phys-ed classes, I tried to exercise as little as possible throughout high school and college.

Then something really weird happened: I was on a business trip in Miami when I was twenty-six and was out for a walk on the beach when these two girls jogged past me. I felt ... jealous. Not of their bodies, but of the running. I'd been in weekly therapy for several months by that time. I was still bingeing at least once a week, but I had sworn off dieting and I was well on my way to a much healthier body image (more on that in Chapters 7 and 8). I realized while watching those girls that I wanted to breathe hard and sweat and move my body. No one was forcing me to do it. It didn't seem like a punishment; it seemed like an opportunity. It actually looked fun. So I went out and bought a sports bra, put on my sneakers, and took a jog that very day.

It felt so good! It was like I had a whole bunch of gunk built up in my brain and joints and muscles and that ten minutes of running just swept it all out. The next morning I woke up and did it again. When I got back to New York, I kept it up, running around my Brooklyn neighborhood for ten or fifteen minutes at a time a few days a week after work, even in the snow. I worked up to a mile, then two miles, then three, then I found myself a running partner. Within about nine months, I could run for a seemingly impossible sixty minutes at a time. Eventually, this led to my training for and jogging the New York City Marathon. When I signed up for it, I remember telling my mom and hearing befuddled silence on the other end of the phone. She actually said, "You can't do *that*!" She was picturing the teenage girl she had to drag to the gym kicking and screaming; the depressed seventeen-year-old who could barely peel herself up off the couch. She didn't really know this version of me yet. She didn't realize how much I'd grown and changed.

Mom wasn't the only one who told me I couldn't do it: I was around 180 pounds at the time, which is a little extra weight for my frame, and running had started to hurt my knees and feet. I went to a podiatrist to get advice and some orthotic inserts for my running shoes, and when I told him I was training for a marathon, he looked at me sort of cross-eyed and said, "Yeah, good luck . . ." Whether it was because of my weight or the condition of my feet, I'll never know. I do know that a couple years before, those comments would've been enough to derail me and send me headfirst into a bag of miniature Reese's peanut butter cups. But I'd already built up such a sense of accomplishment from running three, then five, then six, then eight whole miles that my confidence was unshaken. I was training four days a week and sticking to it, and the sense of accomplishment that came from doing what I said I was going to do (not to mention the crazy endorphin highs) was priceless. My bingeing slowed even further, most likely as a result of my growing self-esteem, sense of personal power, and the stress relief of all that physical activity.

Anna told me that she found training for a race to be a real self-esteem booster, too: "This past fall I used a twelve-week program called 'Couch to 5K' to go from not running at all to being able to jog 3.2 miles," she said. "Building up to a goal I

Bingeing on exercise can be just as destructive and dangerous and bingeing on food.

---

never thought I would be able to do was an amazing experience. I felt strong and more certain than ever that with enough time and work, you can achieve anything you want."

All that said, physical activity is a helpful tool only if we are able to use its power for good, not evil. "I do have to be careful with exercise," Anna admitted. "Physical activity always makes me feel better, but it can be a binge trigger, too. I can often feel like a vigorous workout entitles me to more food than I need. Or, if I'm in a workout routine and I miss a day for whatever reason, I can easily come to the opinion that I've blown my whole healthy lifestyle. I have to really work to have balance around exercise. I try and stick to forms of exercise that are gentle, or that I really love and can build goals around."

The same kind of black-and-white thinking that creeps into our minds about food can make us get weird about working out. Bingeing on exercise can be just as destructive and dangerous as bingeing on food. There's even a type of disorder called exercise bulimia, in which one binges then works out for hours to "purge" the food. That's a subject fitness trainer Kathy Kaehler knows a lot about. She's the author of seven books, including *Teenage Fitness*, and has worked with dozens of celebrities. But she's also the ambassador for the Alliance for Eating Disorders Awareness. Why? Because Kaehler used to be bulimic. She stopped bingeing and purging in her early twenties, but then her disorder basically shifted into an obsessive need to exercise, she told me. "I wasn't realizing that I was compulsively exercising at first, because it ended up being my job," she said. "I wanted to have money, so I was working hard; but that meant I was exercising with clients multiple times a day. There was such a negativity to exercise when I was sick. I thought of it as the killer of calories, the killer of fat." But it's not like that for her anymore—she's found balance and uses her history with compulsive exercise and bulimia to help other people find it, too. "Now I really do enjoy going out and riding my bike, and exercise is something that is a way to make me feel good, a way to make me loosen up my body, a way to nourish my joints and my muscles. It's more of a happy feeling, a positive feeling, an accomplished feeling."

I was never a compulsive exerciser, but I still make a conscious effort never to think about calories or weight when I work out. Putting movement in a weight-control framework instantly takes the joy out of it for me and turns it into a chore. I move my body on a regular basis not to burn calories or lose weight but because it is an ongoing tool that improves my mood, clears my mind, and keeps me feeling connected to my physical body. Like Anna, I tend to do gentle exercise that feels more nourishing than punishing. I do weight training and Pilates once or twice a week, and if I'm in the mood and the weather's good, I'll take a jog around Prospect Park near where I live in Brooklyn or hit the elliptical at the gym. (Oh, and my husband bought me a cute blue bike, so now in the summer, we like to go for long rides around the neighborhood or down to the beach at Coney Island.) Once in a while, if I'm really wound up, anxious, angry, or just feeling mentally clogged up, I'll use more intense exercise—like ten or twenty minutes of fast-paced running intervals—as a strategy to discharge that emotion, like we talked about in the last chapter.

Yoga: The Perfect Exercise for Binge Eaters?

I'll admit it: Yoga's not really my "thing." That said, there is some amazing research showing that doing yoga can help lessen the severity of eating disorders. I know people who have benefited greatly from the sense of connectedness to their body and mind that comes from doing yoga regularly, and for some people it's the ultimate combination of three of the major tools I talk about in this chapter: physical activity, meditation, and spirituality. "I took up yoga and I honestly began to appreciate my body for what it could do," Rachael told me. "The first class I was hopeless—my legs couldn't bend the way they should for poses, but within four weeks I was amazed how much more flexible I became. Yoga is gentle and meditative and I found it really helped me learn to love my body." ✳

Tool: Support

As I talked about earlier, I was doing pretty well by the time I got into my late twenties. The bouts of depression were under control, my self-esteem was stronger than it had ever been, I was doing okay at work, I was physically active, and my weight had stabilized at around 180 pounds. But I was still bingeing an average of once a week—and I ate emotionally fairly regularly. My feelings often still dictated my food choices. If I was overwhelmed at work, I'd have something fried, bready, or "comforty" for lunch. During really stressful times when anxiety, work pressure, or family issues built up, I would wake up in the middle of the night from a dead sleep and eat bread and butter or a few bowls of cereal. There still seemed to be certain foods that I basically had no control over at all, like peanut butter, chocolate, chips, and pizza. I couldn't keep them in my house. One bite of those things and it was binge city.

A couple of months before my thirtieth birthday, I had a bit of an epiphany. I was doing pretty okay, as I said, but I felt an emptiness. I dreamed of being completely free of bingeing. I wanted to really succeed in life, not just get by. I wanted to find a solid, loving relationship and get married. I wanted to have children! Somehow I knew that I personally wouldn't be able to have those things if I didn't finally kick the bingeing. I needed to try something different, something big to get over that last hump. I knew about twelve-step overeating support groups because I'd been to a meeting once way back when I was sixteen. It hadn't felt right at the time—there was no one my age in that group and I simply wasn't ready for a step like that yet— but things were different now. I looked up some meeting times in New York City and worked up the courage to go to one.

The relief I felt being in a room full of people who—despite varying ages, races, body shapes, whatever—were just like me was indescribable. I saw myself in every single one of the stories they told. I saw hope. I saw mentors who could share their wisdom. I saw people I could reach out to when I felt shaky or was about to binge. From that very first meeting, I knew I had found the next tool in my recovery, the next step.

Anna had a similar experience when she started going to a support group for binge eating. "Walking into my first meeting was so incredibly nerve-racking," she said. "But I knew I needed help. I had reached the limit of my capabilities in terms of being able to help myself. I walked into the room and was certain everyone would know I was new and would think I didn't belong, or that they weren't going to understand me or want to know anything about me and my pathetic problem." Those fears started melting away for her once the speaker began to talk and the group members shared their comments. "As soon as I started hearing my feelings come out of the mouths of these strangers, I was able to let my cynical thoughts go ever so slightly. Every single person who talked about their food problems said something that rang true for me. I was floored and I knew that I wanted to glow with the self-love and care that some of those women were exhibiting. I knew that I wanted to stop bingeing, and people in the group let me know it was possible, that they themselves had done it.

Morgan gained insight by going to a group, too. "The support group was the first time that I talked with people other than my own mother about what I was going through. It was helpful to hear other people's stories and experiences and helped me to put a lot of my behaviors into perspective." For a guide to finding a support group in your area, see Support Groups 101 on page 219.

Face-to-face support groups were helpful for me, Morgan, and Anna, but you don't have to walk into a room of strangers if you don't want to do that just yet. You can start out with similar kinds of support online. Take Casey, for instance, who uses my site HealthyGirl.org as her online support group of sorts. I've gotten countless e-mails from girls as young as fifteen and women as old as forty-five saying that they see their own struggles reflected in the blog posts and other stories there. "Knowing that other girls are struggling with this same issue that has shamed me for so many years is a great big relief," Casey told me. "Few of my friends know I struggle with food, and it makes me wonder how many of them are going through a similar situation." SomethingFishy.org also has an incredibly supportive and safe community for people who suffer from any and all disordered eating issues. "I do believe that the more human contact there is, the better," said psychiatrist Charles Sophy. "But sometimes, for some people it only feels safe to go online. It's a first step." (For more suggestions, see Online Resources: Recommended Websites on page 222.) Know that your need and use of a support group of any kind may change over the journey of your recovery. "I was relatively young compared to a lot of members of the group I went to," Morgan told me. "After about four months, I felt a lot better and I stopped going to the meetings. A lot of the conversations had turned into ones about issues I couldn't totally relate to—marriage, having children, older-adult relationships. I could empathize and appreciate what the other members were saying and feeling, but it just wasn't where I was at in my life, so it became a little less relevant to my own recovery. At that point I felt strong enough and in a good enough place with my own self that I thought I could

> Even just telling one other person about what you're going through can be key to recovery.

handle things on my own." Morgan had picked up several other tools during that time as well, including physical activity, therapy, and meditation (more on the last two in a bit), and the group no longer felt necessary for her. Anna, on the other hand, still attends support meetings at least once a week even though she doesn't binge eat anymore. For her, these meetings have become an ongoing, long-term tool for growth and coping with life. "The single-most-important skill I've made use of in recovery has been talking and sharing honestly with other people who understand and struggle with the same issues," she told me. "After a lifetime of feeling so alone in my eating disorder, there is simply nothing like talking with others who know exactly how I feel. It's incredible and can break through my bad moods like no other."

I went to twelve-step meetings regularly for more than three years, and the support I found there was absolutely invaluable. But like Morgan, I no longer attend and now rely more on other tools and find my support mostly through my husband, therapist, and my work with young women at HealthyGirl.org.

There are many ways to get support, whether it's from a face-to-face group, an online forum, or from your doctor, parents, siblings, pastor, husband, boyfriend, girlfriend, best friend, or therapist. All of it counts, and all of it can be used as an ongoing tool to help you cope with life and keep getting better. Even just telling one other person about what you're going through can be key to recovery, Dr. Sophy believes. "Secrets have power," he told me. "You've got to relinquish this to another person. Anyone you can safely and confidentially relinquish it to. Get it safely out of your mind and body and the power, the pressure, of the secret is gone."

Tool: Therapy

I know that therapy is a scary (and expensive-sounding) concept for some people, but therapy has probably been the single-most-important ongoing tool for my growth and recovery. In talk therapy, I have worked through major life issues like the trauma of my parents' divorce, have been able to heal my relationship with both my mom and my dad, and let go of guilt for my own past wrongs. Therapy also allowed me to build the self-esteem I needed to walk into my first support group meeting and finally stop bingeing for good. I'm not saying that everyone who wants to heal from emotional overeating needs to see a professional;

every single one of us is different and so are our recovery journeys. But I will say this: Humans are complicated beings, and we don't come with instruction manuals. There are people out there who study psychology, psychiatry, and eating disorders, and spend years researching and learning about them. Why not tap into that expertise if we can?

Ashley, sixteen, recently took the step of seeking out therapy and is glad she did. "I'm not really sure how I decided to do it. I just began to realize that I really can't handle being too obsessed with food and just being so unhappy all the time," she told me. "There was so much of my energy that was being zapped from counting calories and worrying and not being able to just cut loose. I was feeling exhausted from the fight against myself, so I knew I had to do something. I'm beginning to think more about the reasons behind my eating issues. I am still going through the binges and restrictions, but I have more awareness about them. I notice why I'm thinking about having a binge or why I feel like I want to skip eating for a day. Even just starting to understand why I do the things I do gives me hope that someday I'll be normal about it. I've learned a lot about myself and why I act a certain way even just in the two months I've been seeing a psychologist." Hillary has found some relief and wisdom in therapy, too. "I've only been going for about a month, but already feel that it is helping immensely," she said. "It's made me realize that there are so many underlying emotional issues that are causing the overeating and they have nothing to do with food at all. We rarely end up talking about the eating, but I can already feel a release in tension as I'm able to talk through things that I've always held back in the past."

Razieh, whom we met earlier, also praises the benefits of therapy: "About a year ago, I made the best decision of my life and made an appointment with the therapist I am seeing. Every session I have I become more and more honest with her. I think that honesty is such an essential element of recovery. Even when I know my thoughts seem irrational, I tell her, and it helps me move on."

Finding a therapist isn't always easy, of course. Razieh went to four different people before meeting her current person and deciding to work with her. The first therapist I went to here in New York was sort of stiff and not very relatable, and after a couple months, I realized I didn't like him very much. One of my good friends at work had been open about seeing someone who helped her deal with her bulimia, so I asked for the woman's number. I went to see her, and it was a great match!

Twenty-two-year-old Erica found her therapist through a referral, too: "When I first told my parents that I believed I had binge eating disorder and needed to speak to a professional, my mom asked her therapist if she knew of anyone who specialized in helping people with eating disorders," she told me. "Sure enough, she did, and within a couple weeks I was in therapy with a woman who was really good. Unfortunately, she wasn't covered under our insurance, so my parents and I knew we wouldn't be able to pay for too many sessions. It was also almost time for me to go back to school for my sophomore year, which is about forty-five minutes away from my home, so we figured it'd be better for me to find someone new, anyway. I then went through my school's counseling center, and they were able to match me up with a therapist within the area who did take our insurance and who I met with weekly for about nine months."

Like Erica mentioned, finding the money to pay for a therapist isn't always easy. My health insurance reimbursed me for about half of the cost of each session, which was incredibly helpful. Even so, when I first started therapy, my portion—fifty-five dollars a week—was a big financial commitment for someone on an entry-level journalist's salary. But that's just it: It was a commitment. Therapy was something I decided was so valuable that I was willing to go without other things to get it.

Bobbie, a sixteen-year-old who has been dealing with starving and bingeing for about a year now, told me money was a big reason she couldn't get professional help. But when I pressed her, it turned out there were other, very significant reasons she didn't want to go to a pro: "I've thought about it a couple of times, but there's no way I have the time, money, or courage to do that," she told me. "I don't have the courage to go because I feel like it's such a horrible secret that I don't want anyone to know about me. I don't want people to look down upon me and think, 'There are people in need all across the world and she is shoving food in her face and crying about it? What a disgusting person!' I also feel like the more I pay attention to binge eating and the more I talk to people about it, the bigger a problem it will become. It will make it feel more real."

Feeling ashamed is a common obstacle to asking for help, whether it's from a professional or a friend, said Dr. Michael Lukens. "It's like you can't get past your problem because your problem blocks you getting help," he told me. "You could draw a medical comparison. If you fall off your bike and have lingering pain, you can't diagnose whether you have a broken bone or not all by yourself. Expertise goes a long, long way."

I've seen my therapist as often as once a week at times, or as infrequently as once a month. I don't think I will regularly be in therapy forever, but at this time in my journey, I still find talk therapy with a supportive, educated, objective, and insightful person (who knows me incredibly well by this point) to be valuable.

Therapy 101: What Is It, How Do I Pay for It, and Where Do I Get It?

Therapy can be a scary concept if you or no one else in your family or friend group has ever done it. Here are the basics to help you get familiar with it and get started finding someone.

There are several different types of therapy. **Cognitive behavioral therapy (CBT)**, for instance, has been shown to be very effective for people with bulimia or binge eating disorder—and also in other compulsive behaviors like skin picking or hair pulling. It focuses on impulse interruption and the importance of our thoughts in determining behavior. Much of it often revolves around cognitive distortions like the ones we discussed in Chapter 4. **Interpersonal psychotherapy**, short-term therapy that focuses on how a person relates to other people, has also been shown to be very effective in helping binge eaters get better. There's also **nutrition therapy**, in which a registered dietitian, who is also skilled in talk therapy, works with you to help you get sane about food, and even **guided self-help**, in which you have short sessions with a therapist or social worker as they guide you through the book *Overcoming Binge Eating*, which was written by CBT expert Christopher Fairburn, M.D. The first thing for you to do may be to do a little research and ask yourself what kind of therapy experience you want. Do you want to see a CBT therapist? Do you want to do general talk therapy about life issues like I did? Do you want to seek out someone who specializes in binge eating or other eating disorders such as Dr. Lukens, Dr. Nardozzi, or Dr. Bulik? Do you want to go to an inpatient or outpatient program at an eating disorders clinic such as the Renfrew Center or Remuda Ranch?

To find a good therapist, ask for referrals from friends or

family members who may be in therapy or who have been to someone they like. Their therapist may not take you on—mine doesn't like to treat friends or family members of her current clients—but they have lots of professional friends and colleagues at their fingertips and know who has a good reputation and who doesn't. You could also ask for a referral from your doctor or ob-gyn. Also, see the Resources section at the end of this book for a list of therapist referral services and well-regarded disordered eating treatment programs around the country. If you don't like or click with someone after the first couple of sessions, it is completely within your rights—in fact it's in your best interest—to try someone else. The person may not want to lose you as a client, but a good therapist will always respect your decision to move on to someone else.

If you go to a therapist who is not affiliated with your health insurance plan (there are a lot of psychologists and psychiatrists around the country who don't take insurance at all; none of mine did), you will have to pay the fees up front, then send in your bills and wait for reimbursement. As I mentioned earlier in the chapter, if you're a student, you may also be able to get discounted or completely free therapy through your school's campus psychological or health services.

Tool: Reading

Remember when I talked about Mitch, the counselor whom my mom and dad sent me to for a while when they were divorcing? He's the one person who gave me my first book about emotional eating, *Feeding the Hungry Heart*, by Geneen Roth. Reading that book, I realized that there was a name for what I was doing—compulsive overeating or emotional eating—and that I wasn't simply lazy, crazy, or a pig or a freak. I was doing something lots and lots and lots of other people did: using food to cope with life and my emotions. Reading that book didn't help me stop bingeing, but it was the beginning of my recovery. It helped me not feel so damn awful about what I was doing. After reading about the book on my website, Katherine, twenty-nine, decided to pick up a copy and said it didn't take long to start making a difference for her. "I am halfway through reading *Feeding the Hungry Heart* at the moment," she told me. "Would you believe my thoughts and attitude toward food are already slowly changing? I still get the urge to overeat, but at least for now, I am really trying to change and focus on being healthy rather than on calories and weight."

Hillary also started with one of Roth's books. "*Breaking Free from Emotional Eating* was the first book I read on eating issues," she told me, "and I think it really helped me identify the problem and realize that other women go through the same thing. But it also made me realize that my emotional eating was a problem I couldn't solve on my own and that it would definitely take consistent therapy to help work through my emotions and talk about issues that were specific to me."

Anna has found books to be valuable, too. "Self-help books have been so key in my recovery and growth," she said. "For all of the corny, overly simplistic books on those shelves, there are quite a few absolute miracles in paperback form. Cheri Huber's *There Is Nothing Wrong with You* and Margaret Bullitt-Jonas's *Holy Hunger* were both books that I read early on in my recovery that helped enormously. I also gravitate toward books about addiction. I feel such a relation to addicts and their intense cravings for drugs or alcohol. That's my story with food. I'm the same as a drug addict, but my substance of choice is food. I find reading memoirs of people who have struggled with and recovered from addiction of any kind to be very helpful in learning about the way my mind works in terms of cravings and behaviors. Again, the opportunity to relate to someone about issues and behaviors that feel so utterly unique to me and crazy is such a gift." (For a list of self-help books I love, or that were recommended by young women and experts I interviewed for this book, see Further Reading: Recommended Books on page 221.)

It's not just actual books that are helpful to read. Many of the girls I interviewed told me that they first discovered that they had a food problem by reading descriptions of bingeing, binge eating disorder, or other disordered eating on the Internet. "I haven't read books, but I have read a lot about disordered eating online," Casey told me. "I follow a lot of healthy eating blogs, and they have really helped me to see that there are many ways to eat 'healthy' and still have fun with life. Pressuring myself to be 'perfect' and thus eat 'perfect' is often what causes me to over-eat. It's always a big relief to see my favorite bloggers who have healthy body images and healthy attitudes toward food eat a cupcake every once in a while." A few good sites for information include NationalEatingDisorders.org, AllianceForEatingDisorders.com, and SomethingFishy.org. (For more, see Online Resources: Recommended Websites on page 222.)

Tool: Meditation

I used to think meditation was just plain weird. I grew up in a pretty strict religion, and during the eighties, when my family and I were active churchgoers, the general thought at our church was that anything that wasn't focused around God or Jesus was "fringe" at best and, at worst, actually evil. I don't know what that religion's beliefs about meditation are now, but mine have changed dramatically. I now use meditation a few times a week as an ongoing tool to relax, recenter myself, boost my creativity, calm my mind, process emotions, and even sleep better. According to the National Center for Complementary

One study found that women with binge
eating disorder who took a six-week course
on mindfulness meditation experienced
fewer and less severe binges.

and Alternative Medicine (part of the United States National Institutes of Health), meditation has been a spiritual and healing tool for more than five thousand years. After years and years of historical practice and use in Eastern spirituality and medicine, it's now offered as a mind-body therapy in hospitals in the West, too, as a tool for reducing stress and possibly even lowering the risk of high blood pressure, heart disease, and other illnesses, including eating disorders. One study found that women with binge eating disorder who took a six-week course on mindfulness meditation experienced fewer and less severe binges. The average frequency of the women's binge episodes dropped from four a week to fewer than two. Research has also found that meditation creates real changes in the body and brain. It reduces activity in the sympathetic nervous system, which tells the body it's in danger and produces that heart-pounding fight-or-flight stress response—and it increases activity in the parasympathetic nervous system, which tells the body everything is okay, relaxing the stress response and slow-ing breathing and heart rate. That same study found that meditation increases electrical activity in an area of the brain related to positive mood.

Whatever it does and however it works, I've certainly found meditation to come in handy. My first experience with it was an incredibly simple type of mantra repetition and deep breathing I learned from a mentor in my support group. She did this thing every morning where she sat quietly with her eyes closed for about ten minutes, mentally repeating an affirmation with each breath. When she inhaled she'd think something like *I'm breathing in peace . . .* , and as she exhaled, she'd say to herself, *I'm breathing out anger*. I started doing this for five minutes most mornings—my affirmations usually focused around breathing in calm and breathing out anxiety, or breathing in clarity and breathing out confusion—and the effects were sort of incredible. After just a couple of weeks, my mind started feeling clearer. I felt like I was better able to concentrate at work, and to sort out complicated or confusing emotions. At the same time, of course, I was attending weekly meetings, reading, and exercising once or twice a week. All of those tools put together started changing my life. Not only was I bingeing less, but I was happier, more put together, and more consistent. I started showing up to things on time, I didn't feel the urge to procrastinate as much as I used to and felt generally stronger emotionally. Even an old boss of mine noticed. I remember just a few months after I started using these tools consistently, she said to me, out of the blue, "You've been doing really amazing work lately. I don't know what you're doing, but whatever it is, keep doing it." What a great feeling!

Meditation 101: A Beginner's Guide

There are lots of different types of meditation. Here's a quick overview of a few of the most common practices.

Mindfulness meditation: This is the type of meditation I practice, often using guided meditation podcasts or MP3s. I try to do it a few times a week, often in the morning during my commute to work on the subway, or in the midafternoon on my days off. In these guided meditations, you sit or lie down and focus your attention on your own breathing or sensations you're experiencing in your body. If your attention wanders, you softly bring it back to your breath or body. You don't censor your thoughts, but you let them come and go, not getting attached to them. A sense of being an impartial observer of what's going in your body is important in these sessions. Mindfulness practices and principles can be applied to activities and events in everyday life, as well, whether it's during meals, on walks, or while sitting quietly in the park. The basic tenets are noticing, observing, reflecting, and simply being, rather than doing or reacting. I'll sometimes listen to a guided meditation while walking around the neighborhood and find that it helps me notice and connect with the world around me.

Transcendental Meditation: The ultimate goal in Transcendental Meditation is for your mind to become still and free of thought. It uses a mantra like "Om" or "Mu" that you repeat over and over in order to bring about this mental state. Practitioners often do it twice a day for fifteen to twenty minutes—once in the morning, once in the evening. I've never tried it, but close friends of mine have taken classes and fallen in love with it.

Deep breathing: Some types of meditation can focus completely on controlling the way you breathe, either by inhaling and exhaling specifically from the nose or the mouth, or by doing it very quickly or slowly. Oftentimes, deep-breathing exercises include relaxing the belly and trying to breathe from deep in your abdomen, rather than using the quick, shallow breaths many of us resort to in regular life or when we're stressed. I sometimes do simple deep breathing into my belly—in through my nose and out through the mouth—for three or four minutes during the workday if I find myself feeling crazed.

If you ask me, the kind of meditation you end up doing doesn't really matter. It's whatever works for you, whatever you can make time for, whatever feels safest and most comforting. Anna adapted her own method of meditating: "My form of meditation has always been very simple. I just set my cell-phone timer for around ten minutes and close my eyes. I let my mind wander to positive things, or I focus on my breath, or I have a calm conversation with myself about hope and gratitude."

Tool: Spirituality

I mentioned earlier that I grew up very religious. Despite its strictness, I really loved my church, especially the prayer and music. I remember having several vivid experiences of what you might call divine connection—moments in which I felt very emotionally open and like I was communing with a higher being. It usually happened while singing hymns. Prayer also used to make me feel very safe and helped me calm any anxieties I had about my loved ones being taken care of.

Once my parents divorced, we stopped going to church, and spirituality of any kind really fell out of my life. Then, in high school and college, as I learned more about world civilizations and other religions, I began to doubt that the tenets of the faith I'd been brought up in were correct. Over the years, I've tried

---

> People don't engage in bingeing or starving or purging just for the heck of it. They're feeling a sense of isolation, a void, a sense of unworthiness, and they're filling it up with these other things.

---

going to different churches, but nothing has really felt quite right. Eventually, I admitted to myself that I no longer believed much, if anything, of what I'd been taught, and that left me with a bit of an emptiness. Without a formal religion, I wasn't sure how to fill that need that all of us have for connection with something bigger and more important than ourselves—what Dr. Nardozzi and other experts call spiritual hunger. To address this need, Dr. Nardozzi and her fellow therapists at the Renfrew Center in Florida created a spirituality program several years ago. "Eating disorders are about something that is so much deeper," Dr. Nardozzi told me. "Your soul is trying to tell you something about what you need. The disorder is serving a higher purpose, because people don't engage in bingeing or starving or purging just for the heck of it. They're feeling a sense of isolation, a void, a sense of unworthiness, and they're filling it up with these other things." In her book *Eating by the Light of the Moon*, Anita Johnston talks about the importance of naming our spiritual hungers. What, specifically, is it that we want and need when we feel this void? she asks. Often it's universally "spiritual" things like love, forgiveness, compassion, gratitude, and charity. For me, it's usually connection—to the people I love, to my emotions, to nature, and to the world around me.

So, if you don't have a regular spiritual practice, how do you go about filling this spiritual need? "The way you access your spirituality may be very different from another person," Dr. Nardozzi told me. "For one person it may be reading the Bible and going to a church or temple; for another person it may be communing with nature. I have one patient who feels most spiritual when she's riding her Harley. She feels really free on her motorcycle, really present. It's just her and the bike and nature. Another time she feels very spiritual is when she's writing her music, she's a musician. Another girl started doing yoga, and for her that was really important—that and the idea of connecting to her own intuition.

"To help people get in touch with what might help spiritually, I often ask what the person's passion is," said Dr. Nardozzi. "What did they lose touch with through the eating disorder? One woman used to ride horses all the time. Do you have a hobby? Or a creative outlet like writing, art, or music? Sometimes that's an access to your spirituality. What wakes you up, what makes you feel present? What makes you feel like 'this is really what I'm intended to do and be"? Spirituality is the action of doing things that are good for your soul. It's really an exploration. No one can say, 'Do it this way.'"

For Anna, journaling and making art help her tap into her passion and emotions. "Getting into a creative space is so cathartic," she told me. "My eating disorder was all about not wanting to feel anything. I could eat and be numb or in physical pain that kept me from my emotions. Activities like writing and drawing got me to slow down and get quiet and express what always felt like chaos and sadness in a way that felt gratifying and that I could sometimes share with those around me." Andrea Mitchell, a licensed art therapist and fitness trainer in New York City, explained to me how creativity has helped many of her clients connect with their deepest selves. "The process of making art can be relaxing, but can also be a way of taking the feelings, sometimes painful, that are inside our bodies and putting them on the outside so we are no longer holding them so tightly," she said. "We may feel we need to let go and get messy, so we gravitate toward paint and color. A timid person new to art may gravitate toward a pencil and begin to doodle. One medium I always use to begin a group or to process for myself is collage. The mixture of mediums and techniques such as cutting, tearing, gluing, painting, and coloring works well for most people. It takes away the judgment of being a good enough artist and allows us to find our feelings in the image of others. It also allows us to take these images and cut, distort, rearrange, and play with them until we create what we need for ourselves. It is the perfect mix of control, power, creativity, and emotional release."

I have yet to delve into my own artsy side, but one thing that makes me feel very present, and very connected to the positive energy in the world, is being of service. Through HealthyGirl .org. I've been able to connect with thousands of women at different points in their journey of recovering from emotional eating or binge eating. With each new connection, with each e-mail or comment I read, I feel a sense of fullness and satisfaction. Reaching out to and connecting with the readers there is like the warmth of a hug, and it fills my heart and reminds me of how I used to feel in church as a kid. I find volunteering spiritually satisfying, too. I used to play bingo with elderly psychiatric patients at a local hospital (usually folks who had dementia or Alzheimer's), and although it was sometimes tough, you could see and feel just how much it meant to these folks to have young people around, to have entertainment, conversation, and company—and I always left with a lighter spirit. For a couple of years I also coordinated monthly trips to a bowling alley with autistic students from a local group home. Doing that, I felt that same sense of what I can only describe as connectedness, gratitude, and positivity. Sometimes even making a simple monetary donation to a good cause can feel spiritual.

I'm still not sure exactly what I believe in terms of whether there's a God or not. Sometimes my old black-and-white thinking tells me that I must figure it out right now, but I know that's ridiculous. Just like I couldn't rush recovery, I can't rush spiritual discovery. For now, I try to take whatever opportunities I can to feel that "divine connectedness" I experienced as a kid in church through things like helping others or being in nature. Something as simple as noticing the pink blossoms on cherry trees in my neighborhood in spring, or stopping to watch snowflakes fall down during winter storms gives me an enormous sense of awe—the sense that, wow, there are things going on in this universe that are way bigger than you or me. Instead of making me feel insignificant, it makes me want to jump in and play my part, to add to the positivity and beauty that's all around us if we just stop to notice it.

Even more important, perhaps, than the number of tools you have in your toolbox or which ones you choose is that you use them consistently. One Pilates class or session of meditation may help me momentarily, but it's really the ongoing, regular use of these things that brings a sense of stability to my mind and my life. After years of experimenting, I've found that I am the most sane about food, my body, work, and everything else in my life when I use a minimum of three tools each week: I try to work out twice, meditate three or four times, and get some support (whether it's therapy or from a friend) once. Far from these things seeming like chores or "have-tos," they've become a natural part of my life and something I look forward to. My hope is that you're able to create your own toolbox and that it's as helpful to you as mine has been to me.

Your Turn:

1. What tools do you already use to help you cope with life and feel sane and satisfied? Do you use them consistently?

2. Are there other tools from this chapter you can add to your own toolbox? Which ones?

3. What actions will you want to take in order to prepare to use these tools? Do you need to research a therapist? Call your insurance company or campus psychological services? Find a local support group? Buy a book? Schedule a mindful walk in the park? When can you make time to take these preparatory steps?

4. Can you commit to using one or more of these tools on a daily or weekly basis, and see what happens? What do you want to happen?

chapter seven

Learning to Love Your Body
(or at Least Not Hate It)

I have an automatic sort of "bullshit!" response when I hear someone admonish a woman to "love your body!" Just . . . love it? Like, just stop hating it and start liking it? Okay, sure, I'll get right on that. Trish has a similar reaction: "I've had probably hundreds of people tell me, 'Look within yourself, you're beautiful no matter what size you are, blah blah blah,' and it doesn't sink in," she told me. The truth is, body dissatisfaction is a complex problem that's best cured by action, not platitudes. "I have to try hard not to roll my eyes at oversimplified stuff like that," said Liza Feilner, M.A., an eating disorders therapist and body image specialist at the Remuda Ranch eating and anxiety disorders clinic in Wickenburg, Arizona. If you have serious body image issues, as many disordered eaters do, "you're not going to suddenly have fuzzy, warm feelings about your body. The real way to change your thoughts and beliefs is to take specific actions to counteract them. Loving someone doesn't always mean you have fuzzy feelings for them; it means you've made a commitment to working through the junk and treating them with respect and kindness even when you don't really want to." Are you ready to make that kind of commitment? Let's start with trying to understand where these negative feelings about our bodies actually come from—and what we really mean when we say "I feel fat."

Body Image Quiz

1. Are you happy with your body weight and shape?

yes... 0
no... 2
uncertain/mixed feelings.. 1

2. Have you ever been teased about your body or weight?

yes... 1
no... 0

3. Have you ever dieted?

yes... 1
no... 0

4. Do you worry about your weight and shape?

never 0

sometimes 1

often 2

daily 3

5. Do you think you will ever achieve your ideal body image?

yes 0

no 1

6. Which would you rather have happen:

Losing 10 pounds this year 1

Ranking in the top 10 of your class or career 0

7. Do you eat three meals a day?

most of the time 0

sometimes 1

almost never 1

Add up your points. If you scored fewer than 5, you're on the healthier side of the body image spectrum, and less likely to have bad body image. If you scored 5 to 10, you're on the riskier side and likely to have a harder time accepting your body. ✳

Adapted from *Eating Disorders: A Handbook for Teens, Families and Teachers* © 2003 Tania Heller, M.D., by permission of McFarland & Company, Inc., Box 611, Jefferson, NC, 28640. www.mcfarlandpub.com.

For Women, Body Hate Starts Early

Nearly every woman has struggled with body image at some point in her life. "In our culture, I don't think anybody is immune to negative messages about body, about size," said Dr. Nardozzi. "We don't live in a vacuum. Men and women are all affected to a certain degree. Do all of us have wonderful body image all the time? No. But are you having more days than not that you're feeling really awful about yourself? Is your mood affected? Or are you not going to certain events because of the way you look? Is your eating or body shape stopping you from really being the *you* you know you were meant to be?" That means bad body image has become a problem for you.

How does body hate happen in the first place? Studies have suggested that, just like with binge eating and other eating disorders, there may be a genetic component to body obsession. Our personalities play a role, too: "Most people are fairly unhappy with some aspect of their appearnace, but some people are a little more sensitive than others about these issues," said Tiffany Stewart, Ph.D., a researcher at the Pennington Center in Baton Rouge where she focuses on the assessment, prevention, and treatment of body image disturbance, eating disorders, and obesity. "If you're more sensitive and feel anxious about these issues, you may be more aware of the pressure in your environment to look a certain way. If you're generally anxious or perfectionistic, that has also been linked to eating disorders and body image problems." I've heard some experts describe this type of personality as being "Velcro." Stuff just sort of sticks to us. Imagine a pair of sisters walking down the street. They get called fat by a boy. One of the girls turns inward; she feels hurt and self-conscious, starts wondering if maybe she actually is fat. The other one turns outward, gets mad, calls the kid a jerk, then moves on. Is one of these girls stronger or weaker than the other? No, but the Velcro girl is more likely to have certain problems, like fragile self-esteem and negative body image.

The first time I felt fat—despite having a normal body size—I was around eight years old. But the body hate didn't really get bad until I was fifteen. Yes, that was around the time I started to binge, but the early teens can be a tough time in terms of body image for girls even if everything else is peachy. It doesn't take a genius to figure out why: During puberty, boys' body fat drops to about 12 percent, while girls' jumps from 16 percent to 27 percent. On average, it's normal for girls to gain two-and-a-half pounds of body fat every year during puberty. Our hips broaden in preparation for being able to carry children and we put on the body fat necessary to be able to sustain another little life inside us. These changes should be celebrated rather than decried. But that kind of rapid change can be incredibly difficult to handle, especially since society's messages about what "fat" means are already well ingrained by that time.

Society's Idea of What's Beautiful

Women today are praised and idolized for having a slim, athletic shape; and, whether we want to or not, most of us do expect ourselves to live up to that ideal. "It's somehow embedded in us that it's our job to look good and that we need to meet a certain standard to be acceptable," said Feilner. Interestingly, this isn't just a modern-day problem. Human beings have been looks-obsessed and body-focused for thousands of years. In the ancient Roman comedic play *Eunuchus* by Terence, there's a scene in which the main character talks about the body ideal of the time—and how the girl he's in love with doesn't match up with it:

> She is a girl who doesn't look like the girls of our day whose mothers strive to make them have sloping shoulders, a squeezed chest so that they look slim. If one is a little plumper, they say she is a boxer and they reduce her diet. Though she is well endowed by nature, this treatment makes her as thin as a bulrush. And men love them for that! [... my lady has] unusual looks ... a natural complexion, a plump and firm body, full of vitality.

Thin and boyish may have been all the rage around 170 BC in Rome, but by the time the Renaissance rolled around more than a thousand years later, the ideal body was considerably plumper. The most beautiful women were often considered to be "Rubenesque"—a term that came from the voluptuously round women that appeared in the paintings of Flemish artist Peter Paul Rubens. "That meant affluence, that you didn't have to work outside, and that you had plenty of food," said Feilner. Fast-forward to 1920s America and the boyish look was back: Rebellious young flappers cut their hair short and wore bandages over their breasts to make themselves look slimmer and less girlie. The pendulum swung back again during the "bombshell" 1950s when skinny teen girls actually went on weight-gain diets in order to make themselves look more like Marilyn Monroe. Superthin model Twiggy hit the scene in the 1960s and the body ideal was whittled down once again. Then came the 1990s, when a young Pamela Anderson debuted her first set of implants on the show *Baywatch*—and the societal ideal seemed to become all about big breasts. By the early 2000s, breast augmentation was incredibly common, even being performed on girls as young as eighteen. In the mid-2000s, the ideal swung back to superskinny again with flat-as-a-board fourteen-year-old models walking the runway and celebs like Lindsay Lohan and Nicole Richie shrinking to skeletal proportions.

We've begun to experience yet another shift. We've started to see more diverse body types in ads (like the original Dove "real beauty" campaign), in major magazines, on television shows, and in movies. If the trend toward acceptance of many different body types continues, I believe it will help make our cultural beauty ideals more fluid and less damaging; and so does Dr. Stewart. "We're definitely at a significant juncture," she said. "We're kind of in a position to decide how this goes. I appreciate any publication or media effort that's trying to head in a direction of accepting healthy body sizes as attractive. There's such a role for the media in this. Literally, if tomorrow things changed radically and all of a sudden all magazines were featuring normal-size people and there was different messaging, I predict people would start thinking differently over time. Our own role in this is huge as well. The more we engage in negative talk about appearance, the more we perpetuate these problems in our society."

I believe the changes Dr. Stewart is talking about are happening, albeit slowly. We can help them to continue by supporting fashion and beauty brands that encourage healthier sizing and advertising images, by buying magazines that show a range of beauties and bodies, by watching TV shows that include a diversity of colors and shapes, and by rejecting those that don't.

Most important, we have to start looking beyond body type in ourselves and in others. Rebecca Radcliffe gives this amazing advice in *Enlightened Eating*: "Society may reward us faster for being thin than for being capable, interesting and creative. However, we don't have to accept that as the only way to think about things. We can begin to notice other things about ourselves that we can like. We can tell ourselves we like things about our personalities, values, abilities and behaviors." Whether our society's values end up changing or not, we need to take responsibility for what we ourselves place the most importance in. In the end, it is up to us to learn to celebrate our talents and individuality, and to take the time to remind ourselves (multiple times a day if necessary!) that we are more than our bodies.

Media Images 101: A Quick Reality Check

You've heard about how researchers have sent audio messages and television airwaves into outer space, right? Just in case someone might be listening, I guess. Well, imagine if the only thing a race of aliens had to learn about us were, say, music videos. Would they think all humans could sing and dance? Maybe. Or what if all they had to go on were soap operas? They'd think all of our men were handsome scoundrels and that our women were backstabbing, wealthy sex kittens.

Of course, music videos and TV shows are art, not reality. The same thing goes for the people we see in movies and in the pages of our favorite magazines. "When you're looking at a magazine cover, even though you know it's been retouched, you are likely to still get sucked in for a minute," said Dr. Stewart. "Then you might even say to yourself, 'I wouldn't mind looking like that.'" But we've got to remind ourselves that even the cover girl doesn't always look like that. You probably already know this, but it bears repeating: The woman on the cover of any magazine—or in any advertisement—just went through three to four hours of hair and makeup, may have had a tailor on-site to cut the clothes to a perfect fit on the spot, and had lights shining in all the right places.

Not only that, but photo retouchers often go back over the final images and take out any weird little clothing wrinkles, soften facial lines, and remove skin spots that somehow still managed to get through all that makeup and flattering lighting. Sometimes they may do things like add more hair, whiten teeth, darken makeup, and even manipulate the model's body size or shape to achieve the exact silhouette the art director is looking for. These images—just like painted portraits of wealthy royals during the Renaissance—are truly pieces of art, not reality.

Some publications and advertsiers are more responsible about the types of image-tweaking they do than others, but it's not always obvious which is which. So here's a good rule of thumb to keep in mind when it comes to pictures of models or famous people in ads, magazines, and other mass media: Unless a photo is a part of a news story or other photojournalism piece, a "gotcha" kind of paparazzi shot, or you're told explicitly in the caption or text of an accompanying story that the image has not been altered, it's safe to assume that some level of retouching has taken place. I'm not happy about that, but it's the way things are, and it's important for all of us to know it. When it comes to looking "perfect," life doesn't have to imitate art—in fact, it can't! ✳

Sometimes Body Image Isn't About Your Body at All

Just like emotional eating isn't really about the food, body hate often isn't about our actual bodies at all. It's completely tied up with our emotions, fears, and the messages we got as children and adults about what it means to be "beautiful." Take me, for example. I didn't just want to be slim when I was a teenager because I thought it was beautiful; I thought that I had to be slim and beautiful to be worth anything. As I talked about in Chapter 4, one of my big issues was fragile self-esteem, and it's common for women to take whatever core emotional issues they have going on and foist them onto their bodies, said Feilner. "You can use your body to validate the feelings you have on the inside," she told me. I never felt good enough, so I could point to my imperfect body as proof my feelings were true. "I can think of a patient right now who feels immense amounts of shame about the trauma she experienced as a kid. That is very painful to deal with. It's easier to focus on the shame of the body. 'See, I should feel ashamed, look at me!' I can think of another girl who is really socially anxious. For an anxious person it's so hard to try to figure out why they feel so inadequate and why people don't respond well to them," she said. "If she can blame her body for that, she has a tangible thing that she can look at and say, 'Yeah, that's the reason,' instead of something nebulous like the fact that she feels awkward and uncomfortable around people."

exercise:
the "then what?" game

During one of my interviews with Feilner, we played a game she calls "Then What?" (it's a psychological technique known as the "Downward Arrow"), which is supposed to help you dig down to the real emotions and core beliefs that are driving your bad body image. She asked me to think back to when I was a teenager and answer based on the beliefs I had then, when I thought I had to be thin.

"If you weren't thin, then what would happen?" she asked me.

I'd be rejected, I said.

"If you were rejected, then what?"

I'd be lonely, I said.

"And what does loneliness mean?"

It means I've been abandoned, I said.

Remember what was going on in my life at that time: my parents' divorce. I was, in fact, feeling completely abandoned and lonely during that period. "Your body became a vehicle to manage those feelings," Feilner explained. Now it's your turn. Take a few minutes to think—and write—about what you think will happen if you do or don't live up to your body ideal. Start with a belief you have about your body: What do you think you are supposed to look like? What would happen if you didn't look that way? How would that make you feel? How do those emotions connect with what's happening in your life right now?

Have you ever felt totally fine when you walked out the door in the morning, then found yourself feeling completely fat and ugly later that same day? "On any given day, I would say that my feelings about my body change pretty dramatically," said Jenn. "I can go from feeling confident to thinking that my flabby stomach is the reason that the guy I have a crush on left our IM conversation."

Guy leaves, girl feels rejected, girl feels bad about her body.

Body hate often isn't about our actual bodies at all.

Psychologist Thomas E. Cash, Ph.D., calls this phenomenon the "moody mirror" in *The Body Image Workbook*—basically, our minds translate whatever negative emotion we're experiencing into a judgment about our bodies. These negative body judgments can often serve the same exact purpose as food: distracting us from something else—something scary—that we really don't want to feel. Hating our thighs might not be pleasant, but at least it's familiar.

"I was just talking to a woman the other day who said, 'I've been eating too much, I need to lose weight,'" Feilner said. "I told her, 'You know it's not about that; it's about why you're eating. Your relationship with your significant other is in a really rocky spot, and until you deal with that, you're going to continue to feel this way about your body.' Do you know what she said to me? 'Well, I don't want to deal with that. I'd rather just stay fat and keep worrying about my body.'" At least she was honest about it!

Avoidance isn't the only emotional purpose that body obsession serves. You can't force your parents to get along better, you can't wish your way into making more money, you can't force a

> Weight and body shape is something
> tangible that we feel like we can change
> even if the rest of our lives are out
> of control.

guy to love you, but "you can look at your body and say, 'I can do something about that,'" said Feilner. Focusing on your body gives you a sense of control. Weight and body shape is something tangible that we feel like we can change even if the rest of our lives are out of control. When I found a publisher for this book, for example, and started HealthyGirl.org, my life started getting very busy and exciting. My dreams were coming true, and yet, interestingly, I slipped into a few of the worst body image months I'd had in years. I had all of these good things happening for me, which made that part of myself that still struggles with self-esteem and fear of success squirm. I didn't really notice that anxiety and self-doubt were starting to build up until I suddenly started feeling "fat." It was a wake-up call to do some thinking, talking, journaling, meditating, and just plain accepting. Once I dealt with the real emotions (the fear of success and the anxiety), the feelings of being "too big" started fading away.

That's the positive side of body image disturbances. Once we learn enough about ourselves, these negative thoughts can be really informative and help tip us off that something's not quite right—or that there are emotions floating around that we need to take a break and deal with. Said Ashley: "When I am upset or stressed or when I'm with people who I'm not comfortable around, I start to get really self-conscious. I guess I realized that when I'm doing stuff that makes me happy, none of it matters, but my negative thoughts about my body kinda tell me when I'm in a bad situation."

exercise:
track your negative body thoughts

The next time you have negative feelings about your body, weight, or shape, grab a pen and try this very simple exercise that Feilner uses with her patients.

1. Write down how you're feeling about your body right now.

2. "Try to go back and identify what the triggering events might have been," she said. "How have you been feeling in the past couple of days? Where are you in your menstrual cycle? Are

you getting enough sleep? Are you eating okay? What other things happened? How are your relationships going? You can almost always trace it to something."

Creating Your Own Idea of What's Beautiful

I hated my body as a teenager and felt decidedly uncomfortable in it for much of my twenties. It's difficult for me to remember the worst of it, but I have fuzzy flashes of memories: I remember being in tears in the shower after a binge, trying to wash some of the self-loathing out of me. I can picture myself running my hands over my belly and hips and wanting to scratch at them, wishing I could somehow just cut the pockets of fat away. The only time I really felt good about my body was when I was on a diet, so I dieted off and on for years. But as I reached my mid-twenties after serveral months of theraphy, things started changing and I finally felt good enough about myself—who I really was on the inside—to let go of the desire to be thinner. I was tired of the diet-and-binge cycle, angry at society for worshipping thinness, and pissed off at the diet industry for preying on our insecurities, so I vowed never to diet again. My weight stabilized at about 183 pounds and I realized that if I stayed that weight for the rest of my life, it would truly be okay with me. I felt fine. Pretty, even. I actually really liked my big boobs and my curvy, muscular legs. It was my first experience with true body acceptance, and it felt awesome. Was I "thin"? No. Did I have stretch marks on my arms and belly? Yep. Did I have chiseled abs? Uh, no. But did I care? No, not really. And that seemed to make all the difference.

"Accepting" yourself doesn't necessarily mean you'll never feel bad about your body or weight ever again, or feel pressure to live up to someone else's body ideals—but you've got to start somewhere. Like Hillary, who told me that she's been able to find certain situations where she likes what she sees in the mirror: "Honestly, I feel the best about my body when I'm naked. My body then is just a body, and isn't restricted by clothing that has a number and a judgment attached to it. I don't have to worry about what size jeans I wear, and my body looks good, curves and all, when it's just a body and not a size. I'm pretty accepting of my body when the only person judging me is myself, but once I think about what other people think about my body, what size I wear, how much I weigh . . . that's when I start to feel bad and embarrassed."

It took me ten years, but as I worked on developing my skills and strengths in life, I also managed to replace other people's ideas of what my body should look like with what I thought about it. "Body dissatisfaction is the difference between your perceived current body size and your ideal body size that you would most like to have," explains Dr. Stewart. "When we test people for body image problems, we use a computer program that, using animated people on a computer screen, allows you to select what you think you look like now, and then what you would ultimately like to look like. The discrepancy between those two gives us an indication of how unhappy you are with your body." Interestingly, Dr. Stewart and her colleagues have found that most people select the same "ideal" body, no matter how big they are in real life. "No matter what their age or weight, it seems people still think everyone should look the same," she said. "That's crazy! Our ideals should vary according to our height, our age, our build. Obviously, if your ideal is very far from where you perceive yourself to be, you're pretty unhappy. If you have very unrealistic expectations, you have a lot of feelings of failure. It's not about the way your body looks; it's about the way you look at your body."

I don't think healthy body image means loving everything about our physical selves, or fooling ourselves into believing that every last bit of us is objectively "beautiful." But it is about loving yourself for who you are, recognizing your many positive attri-

It's not about the way your body looks; it's about the way you look at your body.

butes, and eventually learning that looks are not actually as important as you may have thought. Trish told me, "I always see the flaws, but on good days, I just don't focus on them. On a good day, I focus on my better features. I pride myself on my hair—it's chestnut brown and long and naturally pin straight. I flip it and toss it around all day, and I make sure I keep it healthy and soft. I also really love my eyes. They're a hazel color, and they can range from light brown to gold to green all in the same day."

For me, good body image is about honesty, acceptance, balance, and priorities. My shoulders kinda slope forward a little, I've got floppy earlobes, a flat butt, and stretch marks on my belly and the backs of my arms from my years of bingeing. But so what? I've also got great legs, soft skin, long eyelashes, strong fingernails, nice toes, thick eyebrows and cute freckles. More important, this body can run up the three flights of stairs to my apartment without stopping, walk around New York City for hours on end, ride a bike ten miles on a pretty summer day, and will someday (hopefully!) be able to carry and nourish another life. After many years of struggle, of placing too much value on my outsides, I finally believe to my very core that I am more important than the sum of my body's parts. You can, too.

Your Turn:

1. Take the body image quiz at the beginning of this chapter. How did you score? How do you think your life could benefit from building a better body image?

2. Most of us find it very easy to rattle off a list of our "flaws." Now it's time to list your positive attributes. Write down at least five positive things about the way your body looks, five positive things about what your body does, and five positive things about you as a person.

3. Allow a negative thought about your body to come to mind—then gently, easily replace it with one of the positive things you wrote down in exercise two. Was doing this difficult for you? Can do you make a commitment to practice this anytime negative body thoughts come to mind?

chapter eight

Healthy Girls Don't Diet

I n high school, I'd bring a Slim-Fast to school with me for breakfast, trying to be "good," then I'd skip lunch. By the time I got home, I would've gone nearly eight hours without any sustenance at all, and all day without solid food. (I can still picture that stupid Tupperware drink container I would carry those shakes around in. Ugh.) Our bodies and brains tend to use up their energy stores every three to five hours, so it's no wonder that when I got home from a day of deprivation, I would head straight for the kitchen and frantically eat toast, crackers, cereal, whatever I could get my hands on.

As I mentioned earlier, I began dieting at about the age of eight or nine, using my mom's little calorie-counting books. Over the next several years, I tried everything—shakes, bars

---

Can you imagine how good you might feel if you no longer cared so much about weight or your body shape? If you knew that you never had to go on another diet again? How freeing would that be?

(oh, so many bars), meal skipping, prescription diet pills, herbal supplements, Atkins, a doctor-supervised diet, Jenny Craig. While I'd lose five, ten, even twenty pounds sometimes, I'd always end up the same way: heavier, deeper into the bingeing, and more hopeless than I was when I started. But at around age twenty-seven, I'd had enough and I stopped dieting completely, like I mentioned in the last chapter. I hated being stuck in the diet–binge cycle, and I felt like I was simply worth more than that. As you know, by that time, I'd read several books about emotional eating, gotten my depression under control, and I was in therapy. My self-esteem was built up to a point where I had finally become more than my weight. While I didn't always feel pretty or happy about my shape, I stopped obsessing about it.

The relief I felt was immense. Just think about it for a moment . . . after months or years of dieting and body hatred, can you imagine how good you might feel if you no longer cared so much about weight or your body shape? If you knew that you never had to go on another diet again? How freeing would that be? If that's what you want, you can get there.

I used to think that if I stopped dieting, I'd eat myself to death. Without any rules about the food I ate, wouldn't I just stuff myself night and day, become hugely obese, and eventually die alone as a recluse in an apartment I was too big to leave? Actually, no. Quitting diets turned out to be key to my recovering from binge eating disorder and eventually getting to a comfortable body size.

"I think it's incredibly important to stop dieting in order to restore freedom and get back to what we really value," said Juliet Zuercher, R.D., a dietitian in Phoenix, Arizona, who works with emotional overeaters and other disordered eaters. "Dieting is dangerous and it's maddening. It just magnifies an unhealthy relationship with food. Diets are all about imprisonment and making you a slave to a regimen. You're enslaved to an external source that tells you what's okay and what's not okay. It's the opposite of freedom."

The control you feel when you're on a diet may make it seem like dieting is a cure for bingeing, but the fact is, dieting ultimately makes bingeing worse. Pietro Cottone, Ph.D., a food and addiction researcher at Boston University School of Medicine, actually turned normal rats into binge eaters simply by taking away their favorite food. In one part of the experiment, he and his colleagues would let the rats eat some chocolate-flavored chow, then take it away for a few days. After the rats had been denied their favorite food, and the researchers finally did put the sugary stuff back in their cages, the animals binged—eating very quickly and taking in seven times more food over the course of a day than rats who were fed the same chow all the time. Not only did the rats binge eat, but they got anxious and stressed out during the "dieting" days. Dr. Cottone compared the experiment to yo-yo dieting in humans: "A history of dieting and relapse generates anxiety," he told reporters at the time. "The next attempt to avoid junk foods is going to be more painful and stressful than the previous one, and therefore the likelihood of relapse is going to be progressively higher and higher."

Bobbie is a teenage actress. She started dieting and overexercising about a year ago and now feels stuck in a binge-and-restrict cycle. "Before I started dieting, I never had the urge to binge," she told me. "Never! I ate only when I was hungry and stopped before I got too full. It was never a problem for me until

---

The control you feel when you're on a diet may make it seem like dieting is a cure for bingeing, but the fact is, dieting ultimately makes bingeing worse.

I started trying to lose weight. I remember my friend and I made a pact to eat healthy for a month—we just resolved to step away from sweets and fried foods. The day after we started, I started having cravings for things that I never even liked before. The Twinkies sitting in our pantry all of a sudden looked delicious even though I always hated them. I definitely thought that it was strange how I started craving things once I told myself that I couldn't have them." Strange? Nope, it's just biology.

Amy Jaffe, R.D., M.S., a nutrition therapist in Coral Gables, Florida, said dieting has other effects, too. "Some of the physiological consequences of dieting or losing and regaining weight are an increase in fat mass versus muscle mass, increase in fat cell size and number, decrease in metabolism, a decrease in the energy expended in exercise, increase in the time it takes to lose weight, and decrease in the time it takes to gain weight back," she told me. "These are just some of the ways that dieting actually promotes the exact opposite of what people are trying to achieve. It's why 95 percent of diets fail, more weight is gained back each time they end, and in my estimation, dieting contributes more to causing obesity than curing it."

Not only does dieting—and the inevitable rebound bingeing—take a toll on our bodies and health, it hurts us emotionally, too. I felt like a failure every time I "cheated," "fell off the wagon," "gave in," or "blew my diet." That constant "failure" ate away at my self-esteem and my trust in myself.

"For the past six years I have been trying to lose weight,"

Rachael told me. "It has consistently been on my list of New Year's resolutions year after year. I have tried stupid detox programs, soup diets, etc. I have overexercised—twice a day every day. But it backfires because then I feel so much guilt associated with food that I can't even enjoy one simple cookie. If I eat one, I feel dirty and need to eat them all. The aftermath is always the same: sadness, disgust, regret." Sarah, who's now in college, went to a dietitian in high school for professional help in dropping pounds. "I would follow whatever eating plan she would give me and fall off of it by day three," she told me. "I think it made things worse for me because it showed that I didn't have any discipline, and it made me feel like a failure."

When we diet, we set out to do something that is nearly impossible, and then feel like crap when we fail at it. "It's truly a head trip," said Zuercher. "Dieting is an utter failure for almost everybody that does it. For a chronic dieter, you start to feel like sort of a loser, and that infiltrates your relationships, your career, your mood, your attitude toward life."

Perhaps one of the worst things about dieting, though, is that it keeps you living in the future. We think, "When I'm thin, I will be happy;" "After this diet, I'll feel good"; "Once I lose this ten, twenty-five, or seventy-five pounds, everything will be perfect." In her book *Women Food and God*, Geneen Roth said that happiness is not a function of what you look like, or what you have. "I've been miserable weighing eighty pounds and wearing

---

Happiness is not a function of what you look like, or what you have.

---

a size zero. And I've been happy wearing a size eighteen," she wrote. "It's not about the weight. It's not about the goal. . . . Those are fantasies in your mind—and they are all in the future, a future that never comes. Because when your goals are reached, they will be reached in the 'right now.' And in the 'right now,' you will still be you, doing the same things you do now."

Life is what happens this minute, this day, now. If your mind and hopes are all focused on what's going to happen later, what kind of life does that leave for you today? Certainly not the one you deserve.

Let me assure you, giving up dieting doesn't necessarily mean you're doomed to remain overweight or forever feel uncomfortable in your body. Once I got quite far along in my recovery, I did lose weight, and it hasn't come back. That, of course, isn't the point, though. I suppose there may be some people out there who can focus on weight loss and recovery at the same time, but I couldn't. Once I recovered, the weight loss came as sort of a side effect. Only by making it *not* be the point was it able to happen at all.

But What If I'm Truly Obese? Isn't That Unhealthy?

Sure, having excessive body fat isn't good for us. Obesity can put a strain on our joints, our backs, our bones, our hearts—it's not an ideal way to live, in terms of survival and quality of life. But the fact is, your actual level of health and fitness is determined by much more than what you weigh, including how much physical activity you get, the variety of fruits, vegetables, and grains in your diet, and how much body fat has collected deep in your abdomen, around your internal organs. Women who are shaped like pears—with more body fat on their hips, butts, and thighs—tend to have less heart risk, for example, than women who are shaped more like apples, with more body fat around their waists and bellies. Having a waist larger than thirty-five inches means there are fat stores deep in your abdomen that may be putting you at higher risk for heart disease and diabetes.

I do believe there are some people for whom obesity has become such a physiological and psychological burden that they may require medical treatment. If you're truly concerned about your health, you should go see your doctor for a physical. But know this: For a generally healthy young woman, even one who is obese, weight loss is usually not an emergency. The pounds didn't fly off as soon as I stopped bingeing, as much as I would've liked them to. It took me more than ten years to go from 225 pounds—which is clini-

cally obese for someone almost five nine like me—
am now, at a stable, comfortable, and healthy weight.

"People who recover from binge eating disorder will lose weight if they also increase their physical activity, but not necessarily right away," Dr. Bulik told me. "The body craves regularity—regularly spaced meals so that it can predict how much energy it will be able to use. After regulating your eating, it takes a while for your body to trust you again. So it is not wise to expect immediate weight loss when you stop binge eating. But if you stop binge eating, maintain healthy exercise, and eat regular meals and reasonable portion sizes, then your body will start to trust you again. Usually within a year that trust will be rebuilt and your metabolism will start to normalize."

That, indeed, was my experience. Slowly but surely, over the years, the excess weight has fallen away, and with it, any increased risk of disease that I may once have had. ✳

Get Back in Touch with Your Hunger

A lot of us have been bingeing and dieting for so long that we don't have any idea how to eat normally. We may not even recognize what real hunger feels like. When I was deep into the emotional eating, I never gave my stomach or body enough of a break from the constant snacking and/or bingeing to let it get hungry. "Typically, people who have a history of dieting know when they're really hungry and when they're really full," said Jaffe. "But the in-between, the subtle signs, they're not used to paying attention to those."

Erica said both of the therapists she's worked with had her track her food and mood in a journal. "I had to write what time it was, what I was eating, where I was, and most importantly, what I was feeling at the time or my thoughts looking back," she told me. "I cannot emphasize enough how helpful this is, even now. Without becoming obsessive, it's enlightening to be able to look back after a week and think, 'Ohhh, so that's why I ate that, that's the morning I got into a fight with Mom,' or whatever." It helps keep you aware not only of your trigger foods, but of your trigger situations—daily happenings that set you off and make you want to binge—so that you can develop a plan for how to react when these types of situations arise in the future.

One very important note: You're not allowed to beat yourself up with what you document or observe. "One of the rules of keeping a hunger journal is compassion," said Zuercher. "Think of it as data collection. Pretend you're a scientist or a researcher just watching yourself in your life. You want to make it as neutral as possible and not pass judgment. If you binge, you can take a bird's-eye view of everything that led up to that decision." Look at how you were feeling—just before the binge, earlier that day, or even a few days before—that may have had an effect on you. Once you're aware of these things, you can begin to make different choices, said Zuercher.

> ## exercise:
> ## start a food and
> ## hunger journal

I used a food journal early in my recovery to help get in touch with my physical hunger and start to determine what some of my binge triggers were. (Both Jaffe and Zuercher use such journaling with their clients.) For each time you eat or have the urge to eat, write down:

- Time of day (morning, afternoon, middle of the night, etc.)

- What you wanted to eat

- What you ate

- How physically hungry you were on a hunger/fullness scale of one to ten (one being starving and ten being so stuffed you felt sick)

- How full you were after eating on that same scale

- What you were thinking or how you were feeling at the time

Keep this journal for a full week—or at least two weekdays and both weekend days. (You might find it interesting how your eating and urges change from day to night and from weekday to weekend and back again.) Notice any patterns that pop up. Do you tend to get a hankering for food late at night? Do you tend to skip breakfast or lunch, then have a hard time stopping at dinner? This is all good information that you can use to help get yourself on a healthier path. No matter what this journal reveals, do not beat yourself up. This exercise is about observing yourself and starting to gently reconnect with your body and true physical hunger—guilt will only get in the way.

Create a Plan for Feeding Yourself Well

One of the things I noticed in my food and hunger journals was that if I waited too long to eat during the day, I'd end up overdoing it at dinner, and it would often spiral into a full-on binge. "My first year of college, I would skip breakfast and sometimes not eat my first meal until two or three in the afternoon, and then, of course, I would wonder why I was feeling perpetual hunger or why I couldn't stop eating once I started," Casey told me. Trish has noticed the same thing: "If I'm at school and running around all day, I often completely forget to eat," she told me. "Then, when I get home, and sit down on the couch for a hot second, I realize how hungry I am and end up bingeing. The thing that has really helped me is to pack lunches and prepare meals in advance so that when I'm running around, I don't forget because I have lunch and snacks right there with me."

Making sure I fed myself well throughout the day was key for me. Many people in my support group advocated having a "food plan"—sort of an outline of the way it felt right for you to eat. Some people in the group would eat three meals a day, others ate six small meals, some ate three meals and two snacks, etc. It made sense to plan out meals and snacks so that I wouldn't be caught unprepared, so I decided my plan would be three meals a day, with a snack in the afternoon (I always got hungry before dinner) and a dessert or snack before bed. My body began to balance itself out quite well. I was hungry at meal and snack times, and began seeing even more clearly than before what the difference was between emotional hunger and physical hunger. Three meals and two snacks a day turned out to be plenty of food for my body. So if I wanted to eat more often than that, it was likely for emotional reasons, or it was what Jaffe calls "mouth hunger"—just wanting the taste of something. Sometimes I'd still choose to eat when not hungry, and once in a while I still full-on binged, but most days I ate my three meals and two snacks, felt well fed, and started gaining more clarity around food and in my life in general. I started trusting my body, and my body started trusting me.

When I first made the food plan I talked about above, it included any and every food out there. Part of my healing and saying no to the diet mind-set was letting go of my beliefs that there were "good" foods and "bad" foods. I had no restrictions. As for portions, I simply aimed to eat amounts of food that a normal eater might consider "reasonable." Knowing, as I did, that normal eaters often don't finish all the food on their plates at restaurants, I would look at my plate before I began eating and decide how much of it looked like a "reasonable" serving. Sometimes I'd stop at that reasonable amount, sometimes I didn't, but I tried to be compassionate and easygoing with myself about it no matter what. I knew that if I was too rigid about this new way of eating, I was doomed. I had dessert every single night. Often it was an ice cream bar or serving of frozen yogurt, but sometimes it was a big piece of red velvet cake.

After about a year of doing things that way (and, of course, continuing therapy and going to support meetings every week), I was bingeing so rarely—maybe once or twice a month—that I considered myself recovered from binge eating disorder. It had been four years since I started therapy, about three years since I quit dieting, and a year since I started going to support meetings and taking care of myself with my "food plan." I felt really solid and strong. I didn't hate myself, I didn't hate my body. But my body did feel a little sluggish, and heavy, like the pounds I was carrying just weren't quite right for me. I was working as a health editor at *Glamour* magazine at that time, and they were looking for someone to follow the magazine's nutrition and workout plan and blog about it. I'd been integral in creating the program, worked very closely with the dietitian and trainers who advised us on it, and I knew that it was a nutritionally healthy and sane approach. So I volunteered. I liked the idea of sharing what I'd learned about nutrition and emotional eating with thousands of women online; and, yes, I liked the idea that I might get to a healthier, more comfortable weight.

I still followed my food plan of eating three meals and two snacks a day, but I made tweaks to what was on my plate. Most of the changes I made were shifts to more nutritious and whole foods and fewer processed, packaged foods. I cooked more and ate out less. I made sure that I had a fruit or vegetable at every single meal and snack, and that I ate a combination of protein, carbohydrates, and fats at every meal. I still had dessert every night, but it was usually something small like an ice cream sandwich or a serving of light ice cream with a small cookie or two. Because I no longer had my self-esteem all wrapped up in the outcome, because I no longer beat myself up for sport, because I was no longer actively binge eating, because I had built a toolbox for myself of support meetings, therapy, meditation, and physical activity, I was able to step on the scale, look at the calories on labels, and make changes that allowed about twenty pounds of weight to come off. If it wasn't for the years of preparation, there's no way I could've done it without flipping out and eventually bingeing my face off.

That said, my life and my relationship with food still wasn't where I needed it to be. I was still bingeing once in a while, and I still thought about food more than I wanted to. There was a little more work to be done, and I knew it. Over the years, I'd learned that it wasn't a good idea for me to have finger foods like chips, crackers, and cookies in the house; sugary cereals were also difficult for me to handle, as were chocolate and peanut butter. I didn't keep these items in my house, but I did eat them when I was out at restaurants or with friends. People in my support group talked a lot about "trigger foods"—things that always seemed to lead to a binge. Quite a few of them had given up these trigger foods and found peace and healing in doing so.

"I believe trigger foods exist," said Jaffe. "At times in recovery, avoiding trigger foods may be recommended in order to help a person keep themselves safe from acting out. Then slowly, you can introduce those things back into the person's life as food choices."

I choose what I put in my body . . . I choose
what I value, not an outside diet or how
my body looks. I choose what's defined
as healthy. I choose to take control internally,
to take it all back.

Giving up anything sounded superscary, but I felt like I had the distance from my "dieting" years and the personal strength to try it. So I slowly began to let go of my problem foods. First I stopped eating candy, cookies, and chocolate; then chips, french fries, and pizza; then crackers and peanut butter. Because I was doing it to explore healing, and not to drop pounds or punish myself, it didn't feel like deprivation—it felt like exploration and discovery. I stayed away from those foods for about a year, and I believe that being away from them for a little while was helpful in reducing the amount of time I spent thinking about food, and helping me further avoid binges. It's not a necessary step for everyone, but it did help me.

Then, as I continued healing, I began to feel it was time to add those things back into my life. So, slowly but surely, I started eating pizza again, and peanut butter, and crackers, and chips, and even chocolate. Now, nothing is off-limits, and none of these formerly problematic foods trigger binges anymore.

"I'm all about that pursuit of having the freedom to say, 'I choose what I put in my body,'" said Zuercher. "'I choose what I value, not an outside diet or how my body looks. I choose what's defined as healthy. I choose to take the control internally, to take it all back.' I think we all have the necessary tools and skills to self-regulate."

I have a kind of freedom around food now that I never thought would be possible. I am not exaggerating when I say that I had a box of See's Candies chocolates in my desk drawer at work that I forgot about for weeks. (Miraculous!) Last year, for my birthday, I decided that what I really wanted was for my husband and me and some friends to go to my favorite Mexican place for margaritas and nachos. Nachos used to be a destructive, scary, and forbidden binge food—now they are a crunchy, rich, and delicious food that I eat once in a while when I get a hankering. (Amazing!) Let's see, what else? There are two boxes of crackers in the cupboard, sugary Popsicles that have been in my freezer for a month now unopened, and there's the jar of peanut butter that has lasted for four weeks and counting. Oh, and for my afternoon snack, I just had coffee and a brownie. (Yummy!) These are all things I never thought I'd be able to do. Trusting myself, my cravings, my hunger, and my recovery feels wonderful. And I want you to get there, too.

Eat a Balance of Foods

I did just have a brownie, but of course I don't eat brownies every single day. Why? Because that's not what my body wants. I feel my strongest, healthiest, and most satisfied when my meals and snacks contain a combination of carbohydrates, protein, and fat. Carbohydrates (which are found in grains like rice and wheat, potatoes, sugars, bread, pasta, and beans) are the body's preferred energy source, said Zuercher. Our brain, muscles, and heart rely on glucose (energy) from carbs to keep thinking, moving, and pumping day after day. Protein (found in meats, fish, poultry, eggs, cheeses, milk, yogurt, tofu, some grains like quinoa, nuts, and beans) builds and repairs your body on the cellular level, everything from your muscle fibers to your hair, skin, and nails. "Protein is the stuff your body is made of," said Zuercher. Not only that, but it's complex and takes a while for your body to break down, so it helps slow digestion and, in combination with some carbohydrates, gives you a nice, level source of energy that lasts for a while. Fats are the most complex nutrient, "and they take the longest for the body to break down and digest," said Zuercher. That's why getting a little bit of fat (from things like oil, butter, cheese, meats, dairy products, nuts, and avocados) makes you feel so full and satisfied; it further slows digestion and stretches out the amount of energy you'll get from eating. Not only that, but there are certain vitamins—A, E, D, and K—that are fat soluble, meaning your body can absorb them only if you have enough fat in your diet. Another important reason to eat fat: Getting enough fat in our diets—especially omega-3 fatty acids, like from some nuts, oils, and fish—is incredibly important for keeping our brains in working order.

In addition to having a little carbs, protein, and fat at each meal, I try to have fruit or vegetables with every meal. Fruits and veggies, aside from having a ridiculous amount of vitamins and antioxidants, are also packed with fiber—something that helps protect your digestive system and ward of cancer and heart disease. A perfect example of all of this combo of carbs, protein, fats, and fruits or veggies that I aim for is my favorite after-dinner snack: Greek yogurt with frozen blueberries, a few walnuts, a sprinkle of high-fiber cereal or granola, and a little honey, agave nectar, or maple syrup. Even when we have ice cream in the freezer or my husband brings home cupcakes, sometimes I still choose to have my yogurt concoction. Why? Because my body wants it! And after all these years, I finally trust my body to tell me what I need. Sometimes I need a brownie, sometimes I need an apple. Either way, that's what I give it.

You really can get to a point where you can feed yourself what you want, knowing that your body has the wisdom to balance it out. Casey has gotten there: "I eat well-balanced breakfasts, lunches, and dinners—something that's nutritious but also really tasty, because if I don't love what I'm eating, I'm not going to be satisfied," she told me. "I've learned how to eat and enjoy vegetables. Even more importantly, though, I've learned that I can eat a few slices of pizza without falling down that all-too-familiar 'all-or-nothing' spiral."

Erica is slowly but surely learning to feed herself well, too. "I believe I'm at the point in my recovery where I can focus not only on not bingeing, but also on eating as healthily as possible, like trying to get lots of fruits and vegetables," she said. "But the most important thing for me is to stay away from that all-or-nothing, black-and-white thinking; if I have a big slice of cake,

---

You really can get to a point where you can feed yourself what you want, knowing that your body has the wisdom to balance it out.

---

that doesn't mean I'm 'bad' and that I should say 'screw it!' and eat everything else in sight. Whether I have a small indulgence or an outright binge, my main goal is to stop feeling sad and guilty about it. I feel as though I am treating my body with the respect that it deserves, and I end up loving myself that much more for it."

It's also important, said Jaffe, to eat mindfully. What that means: "Eating slowly, really tasting your food, finding the pleasure in it, because eating is pleasurable," she said. Experts say that it takes an average of about twenty minutes for our stomachs to send our brains the signal that we're full. So, if we're shoving in food like most of us do when we're bingeing or emotionally eating, we're bypassing the delicate hunger system in our bodies that naturally tells us when to stop. We're overloading it, and, perhaps, worst of all, not even enjoying all that delicious food! I have more fun and delight eating two pieces of Neuhaus chocolate (the Caprice ones are my favorite) now than I ever did when I'd eat half a family-size bag of miniature Reese's peanut butter cups.

Amazingly, when I take it slow and enjoy the smell, feel, and taste of each bite, I can eat two chocolates, or three-quarters of a piece of cake, or one serving of ice cream, and feel satisfied instead of obsess about getting more. Part of eating mindfully is also trying not to do other stuff while you eat. How can you fully concentrate on your grilled cheese sandwich or yummy chicken salad if you're also working, studying, or clicking around? "I try to separate mealtimes and homework times," said Trish. "I have learned that time management becomes superimportant when learning to control binge eating—separating the time I eat from the time I do work lessens my chances of blindly putting food in my mouth."

Give Yourself a Fighting Chance!

Binge eating isn't just about our feelings. As we discussed in Chapter 3, for some of us, this problem is genetic. For all of us, this behavior has become deeply ingrained in our brains through repetition. Binge eating has become a habit, and completely apart from our emotions, certain situations can trigger it. David Kessler, M.D., former commissioner of the Food and Drug Administration and author of *The End of Overeating*, struggled with food obsession and overeating for many years. He has found in his research and personal experience that the urge to binge is sometimes based on memories—anything from the time of day to where you are. "You'll walk down the street and start thinking about chocolate-covered pretzels because you've had them before on the same street," he told *Health* magazine.

So true! Certain foods may not trigger binges for me anymore, but to this day, eating straight out of a box or package makes me feel weird. It's like I'm transported back to all the times I stood at the kitchen counter shoveling handful after handful of cereal into my mouth or mechanically eating chip after chip until a bag of Doritos disappeared. Reaching my hand into a box of cereal triggers that history of compulsive thoughts and actions that still, despite my years of recovery, reside deep inside my brain. So, to give myself a fighting chance, I try to avoid eating straight from packages, and usually put my food in a bowl or on a plate or napkin before digging in.

Another situational trigger I have learned to watch out for is watching TV alone on the couch, late at night. I binged that way hundreds of times over the years, and every once in a while, if I'm watching something late at night, my thoughts turn to food. To give myself a fighting chance, I try to avoid being on the couch alone after ten p.m. If I want to watch TV and my husband has already gone to bed, the smartest thing for me to do is bring my laptop into the bedroom and watch with my headphones on. Other situational or "habit" triggers I used to have— like eating as soon as I got home from work, or a party, or whatever—have completely faded away.

Know That the Way You Eat Will Change Again and Again

Part of me didn't want to write about my weight loss or about cutting out trigger foods, because I don't want any of you to get the idea that thinking about calories or cutting foods out of your diet is the answer. I had years of therapy and recovery under my belt before I tried to lose weight in a healthy, sane way, and I had a ton of support and mentorship from people in my meetings when I decided to avoid trigger foods. Recovery is a winding road and my food plan and eating habits have morphed countless times over this journey. Please, keep in mind that everyone's recovery is different. Just because this is the eating path I followed doesn't mean it's the one you should follow. Reading this book, journaling, getting in touch with your hunger, making your own food plan are all amazing steps that will move you along in your recovery, but please, whatever you do, don't use my eating history or advice as your only guide. A nutrition expert who is well-versed in working with disordered eaters, like Jaffe and Zuercher, may be able to help you figure out what will work best for you.

The way I eat now is not the way I ate three years ago, five years ago, fifteen years ago. So be prepared for the fact that the way you eat, what you eat, your body shape, weight, nutritional needs, cravings, and triggers are all likely going to change—more than once—over the course of your recovery. Change isn't easy for me, but it's something I've had to become more comfortable with as I flow along with life. "You gotta have the courage to hang in there," said Zuercher. "In spite of feeling uncomfortable. And it's gonna be uncomfortable before eating becomes a happy or natural thing for you again."

Natural—that's a good word for where I'm at now. I've learned to trust life, and myself, knowing that as long as I put one foot in front of the other, use the tools in my toolbox, feed myself well, and do things that continue to help me grow as a person, I will be okay. No, more than okay—I'll be happy and healthy and, most wonderful of all, free.

Your Turn:

1. Write down a quick dieting history—all the times you've dieted or restricted in order to lose weight or try to control the bingeing. Now answer this question: If dieting or restricting worked, why would you have to keep doing it?

2. Are you afraid to stop dieting? What are you afraid might happen? Do you believe that diets actually trigger binges, the way Jaffe, Zuercher, and I say they do?

3. Are you willing to stop dieting if that's what it takes to focus on your recovery from emotional eating and bingeing?

4. Most of us have situational or habit triggers for binges. What are some of yours? Drinking? Coming home and being alone? Watching TV? Can you commit to giving yourself a fighting chance by trying to avoid some of these situations or plan for them in advance?

part three:
living your life without
relying on the good
girl's drug

chapter nine

How to Deal with Friends, Loved Ones, and Food Pushers

As much as we'd like to think we can keep our eating issues just between us and the Oreos, other people are involved in all of this. The people we live and work with, our friends (or frenemies), the guys or girls we date or marry, our parents. After all, part of the reason I wanted to get better was so that I could have better, closer relationships with people. Food had served to keep me just a little bit separate, a little bit out of reach. My bingeing was like a thin, clear film that sort of fell over everything and made me experience all of my emotions—including love and friendship—a little less vividly. That's sad, because what we all need in order to be truly happy is to be vulnerable and connected. This relational stuff isn't the only way food is involved in our dealings with other people, of course. Not only do we share our hearts, our time, and our lives with them, we often have to share refrigerators, cupboards, and actual meals with them, too. That, as any one of you knows, can be tough. Let's talk about how to deal.

Food and Your Friends

When I was in my teens, my mom and my counselor knew that I was binge eating, but there was no way I was going to tell any of my friends about it. I'm sure I wasn't the only one dealing with debilitating body hate and food issues, but I felt like I was. The realization about my food problem was much too new, I was way too ashamed, and in all honesty, my friend group was much too young and gossipy. Although shame and secrecy can be destructive, we don't have to bare our souls to people we don't trust.

Morgan decided to seek out a support group rather than talk to her pals about this issue. "I didn't totally know how to talk about it with my friends, and I also didn't want to be 'eating disorder girl,' and feel like that defined who I was," she told me. Rachael, on the other hand, has shared this part of her life with several close friends. Not all of them understood, but they were kind and tried to be supportive. "For years it was my secret; I felt so strange and disgusting. It has only been the last few months that I have opened up about it," she told me. "I was explaining to a lovely friend the other day what binge eating disorder is and how I have struggled with it for about five years now. She just didn't understand—could not fathom why anyone would want to eat skim-milk powder from a packet or fifteen slices of bread covered in Caesar salad dressing. I replied, 'I don't *want* to,' to which she said, 'Well, why do you do it?' I told another two friends—they knew I had issues with food because I would never eat out at restaurants and was always trying to lose weight, but they had no idea how depressed I was and how much I struggled. It feels okay to have told them, but I still feel a little judged because they just don't understand."

Rachael has also shared with someone who does get it. "I became very close with one friend, and I noticed she had similar issues—I had seen empty containers of food in her room and other things," she said. "We began talking about it openly and that has been a huge help. Though sometimes I think we encourage each other instead of helping: 'I ate a huge block of chocolate yesterday' . . . 'So what—I ate potato wedges with sour cream and a pizza.'"

One of the toughest things about dealing with friends often isn't the decision of whether to tell or not to tell—it's trying not to get sucked into their issues with food or their bodies. I remember when I was around twenty-five, I was on a trip with several other girls, and we were all getting ready to go out to kind of a fancy club. One of them (arguably the slimmest of all of us) simply would not stop body bashing herself. I engaged in the discussion, trying with the others to convince her that she wasn't fat—then I spent most of the night feeling fat myself. If someone as thin as her with clothes as cute as hers hated the way she looked, what must *I* look like, I thought? Looking back, the best thing for me to do would've been to remove myself from the situation by going to get an iced coffee or taking a walk. I could've also taken the brutal honesty tack and said something along the lines of "I understand what you're going through, but can we please change the subject? It's starting to make me feel badly about myself, too." Razieh does her best to skirt situations like this completely: "I try to avoid talking about eating with friends because I know a lot of them also have destructive habits with food and hearing them does not help me improve my recovery," she told me. Smart!

Anyone who has lived with other girls knows that this can be tough, too—not just because it puts us in close contact with them and their possible food and body issues, but also because we have to share cupboard space. I was pretty open about my food issues with my first roommate in New York City. We were friends from college and had moved east from California together. I trusted her completely, and it felt good to be so open with a peer. I don't remember ever stealing any of her food when I was in binge mode, but my next roommate . . . well, I finished off a few of her boxes of cereal and jars of peanut butter. We were friends, and I was open with her about my struggles, and usually replaced what I'd taken. It would've been much harder, I think, if I had to try to hide what I'd done like Amanda did when she shared a bedroom with five sorority sisters in college:

"For me it was horrible. Living in the sorority house, food that wasn't healthy was always available. Many of the girls I was around had unhealthy relationships with food and their bodies, which made my obsession with my looks and insecurities even worse. No one ever walked in on a full food binge; luckily I had been pretty stealthy. If it was the daytime, I would walk to the student union, pick up food, and then go find a quiet area to eat it and walk back. At night, I would wait until all of my room-mates left and would go get food and then eat it alone in my room."

When it comes to friends, many of us also have to navigate a bit of peer pressure to eat. Everyone's having birthday cake, shouldn't you? Everyone's ordering pizza after going out to the bars—it'll be weird if you don't join in, won't it? Casey has figured out a way to deal with this that works for her, and might for you, too. "I don't love the way sugar makes me feel, and if I ate every cupcake, cookie, or candy bar that was passed my way, I would feel icky all the time," she said. "If I truly want something, I'll eat it. I've learned, though, not to sacrifice my own well-being just to take a bite of someone's baked good. I've had great success with the phrase 'This looks so delicious! I'm

---

To all of those who have to deal with
food pushers, polite refusal and standing
your ground in a respectful way is your
best defense.

---

going to save it for dessert." And then, when dessert rolls around, and I decide I no longer want it, I'll give it to someone who does. I'm a very honest person, but I can support a white lie when it comes to food flattery. Go ahead and tell your friend that her chocolate chip cookie was the best chocolate chip cookie you've ever tasted. She'll never know."

Elisa Zied, R.D., a dietitian in New York City who deals with a lot of young women, simply recommends polite refusal when someone offers you food you don't want or don't feel comfortable eating. "I was overweight as a teen and young adult and have learned over time that most who push food don't do it to sabotage you, but do it unknowingly because they equate food with love," she told me. "I accept and understand that, but know that when I overdo it I do not feel comfortable, and won't eat something just because someone begs me or because it's the polite thing to do. To all of those who have to deal with food pushers, polite refusal and standing your ground in a respectful way is your best defense—and your body will thank you."

Should You Tell People You Date About Your Food Issues?

My husband, John, has known about my history of binge eating disorder since before we started dating. We were friends first, and we met when I was already in my midtwenties and on my way to recovery. But that doesn't mean that food hasn't been a point of contention for us a few times in our relationship. He's a normal eater with a big appetite and a hearty sweet tooth, so there have been plenty of times when my particular nutritional needs have caused friction.

For a while, for example, I wasn't comfortable eating pizza. Man, did he hate that. Pizza is one of his favorite foods (and it's actually kind of a special food in our relationship: We ate it next to a lake in Reykjavik, Iceland, the night he asked me to marry him). I remember one night a few years ago, he was craving it, so I told him to go ahead and order it, and that I would have something else. It seemed perfectly reasonable and fair to me, but I remember him looking pained and saying something like "It's not as fun to eat things alone. Are you telling me we're never going to be able to eat pizza together again?" I told him nothing was forever and asked him to be patient. He nodded and tried to be supportive, but I could tell that he really was frustrated about how my issues were affecting him. What finally got him to understand, I think, was when I asked: "Would you rather I go back to the way I used to be when I was bingeing and depressed? Or would you rather eat pizza alone for a little while?" Of course he wanted me to continue to get better, and me sort of laying it out like that helped him put it in perspective. Pizza, no matter how "special" it is, is still just food.

There have been other times when we've had to negotiate what foods to buy or not to buy. I went through a period of a few months when I felt very vulnerable to peanut butter and crackers, for example, two things he likes very much. I explained to him that eating them triggered strange feelings for me and I felt vulnerable having them in the house. He agreed to stop buying them for a while. Then, when I started feeling stronger with it, we'd buy them, but he'd keep them in his home office instead of our main cupboards. Now they're back in the kitchen—I'm at a point where he can keep whatever he likes in the house, including Cocoa Puffs, peanut butter, crackers, pizza, whatever!

I never felt the need to tell guys I dated for a short time about my food issues, but I believe that being open about this part of your life with a person you're seriously dating is important. "I was with my boyfriend from fifteen to nineteen years old and sometimes I would avoid spending a night with him, coming up with an excuse like schoolwork," Rachael told me. "Really I would be eating in secret in my bedroom. He was often offended when I didn't want to spend time with him, and we fought a bit over this, as I did it quite a lot. I was also quite unpredictable—some weeks I would have mostly good days and enjoy having sex, so on those weeks we would have a lot, and then all of a sudden I would 'hate it.' Get angry and upset. Cry when touched or just avoid seeing him so it never came up. I know it hurt him a lot to be constantly rejected and he thought it was something to do with him and it put a huge strain on our relationship."

Opening up and explaining what's going on with you can actually help keep your relationship strong. "My boyfriend was the first person I told about my binges," twenty-four-year-old Jenelle told me. "It took me almost a year to finally tell him why my moods were so up and down—usually on days I binged—and why I don't like being alone in my apartment, often staying at his place, where I seem to have self-control. I was nervous, but once I opened up I felt a huge relief. I thought he'd think of me as broken or damaged when I told him, but the opposite was true. He accepted it as part of me, offered his support, and encouraged me to seek help if it really bothered me. For that, and lots of other things, I really love him and know he really loves me."

Dr. Nardozzi has some patients who actually bring their significant others into therapy sessions. "One girl's boyfriend was telling me that they got these cookies as a gift, and within twenty-four hours, all of them were gone," she said. "The guy said he went to get a cookie and was, like, 'Hey, where are they? What's going on?!' The girl was so shamed by it all and he didn't know what to do. He didn't want to say anything because he was so afraid to say the wrong thing. So we talked about how they could open up the communication so that there would be freedom for him to say something like 'Are you okay?' if he noticed that she had been overeating. Then she could take that opportunity to open up and talk to him, say, 'I'm really anxious and am eating out of anxiety.'"

You do have to set boundaries, though. No one wants their significant other to become the food police or overly involved. John and I had a situation sort of like that come up not too long ago. When I first started writing this book, I was feeling kind of exhausted and raw from the process, and one night I ate some ice cream after John had gone to bed. I wasn't hungry, and I'd already had my bedtime snack, so it was definitely emotional eating. I told John about it the next day, because I knew he'd notice the container was emptier than before and I didn't want him to wonder if I was okay. I knew that even completely normal eaters emotionally eat sometimes, and that as long as it didn't become a habit and I kept using my tools, I'd be just fine—but John got a little freaked out and worried. He said, "Isn't that a binge?!" "Well, technically, I guess you could call it that," I answered. He looked confused and said, "But isn't a binge bad? Isn't that something you shouldn't do?" I said, "Well, it's not ideal, but you don't have to worry about me. I'm not going to go back to having an eating disorder. Even completely normal eaters stress-eat once in a while." He felt better, and so did I.

Dealing with Loved Ones
Who Don't Get It

My mother and I are really close. But as I've talked about, food and weight issues used to cause quite a few fights and hurt feelings between us. When I was a teenager, she'd make comments about what I was eating and give me dieting advice, and I often felt like she was looking over my shoulder. That, it turns out, is not unique. So many of the young women I interviewed for this book told me stories about their moms or dads saying hurtful things about their weight or trying to control what they ate. "I've told my mother before how painful it is when she tells me I'm overweight, and she's gotten better, but still lets hurtful comments slip here and there, like 'Do you really need that? You shouldn't still be hungry,'" Hillary told me. "I can tell that she is constantly holding back from saying more, which is equally hurtful because I know that my weight still bothers her. Despite this, we get along well, and I'm really tired of this coming in between our relationship, because I do really love her. She knows I have an unhealthy relationship with food, but I haven't yet told her that I have binge eating disorder."

Even if you have parents who are relatively well informed about disordered eating issues, talking with them about it can be tough. After all, what loving parent wants to sit back and watch their child harm themselves with binge eating? "Somebody's got to say something," said Dr. Lukens. "But parents are often walking on eggshells—they feel powerlessness, frustration, they're scared, they don't know what they're doing. I've coached parents for hours before sending them out to talk to their child about eating issues."

Rachael lives with her father and said he knows a little bit of what's going on with her, but tends to say just the wrong thing at the wrong time. "I asked him to stop bringing junk food into the house and at first he did, but slowly he started bringing it back in," she told me. "He says things like 'I saw you got into the chocolates,' or 'You really wolfed those down,' which really hurts me. I cried to him and said, 'I really have a problem, Dad. I don't have a normal relationship with food. When you see me making pancakes, I don't enjoy that. I'm doing it simply to eat the whole batch.' The other day I was making something and he said, 'So you're cooking, does this mean you're depressed again?' Tact isn't his strongest point."

Rachael's dad is trying to connect with her. He's trying to start a conversation about what she's going through, but he literally doesn't know what to say. That happens a lot, said Dr. Nardozzi. "I remember one of my patients. Her mother clearly knew she was bingeing, but instead of the mom saying to her, 'I'm really concerned about your behaviors and what's going on,' she'd say, 'You left so many dirty dishes in the sink!' She's worried about her daughter, but she doesn't know how to approach it. She's worried that her daughter won't be receptive to a real discussion. Sometimes people in your life, when they're making comments, it's not out of malice. They may just have no idea how to support you right now."

Imagine how frustrating this could be for your mother or father (or your sister, brother, or friends): knowing you really do need help, but not knowing how to give it to you. "When we're four years old, we're pretty simple—you fall down and hurt your knee, your mom kisses your boo-boo, you're better," said Dr. Lukens. "By the time we're teenagers, we're very complex creatures. In the end, what you usually need from them isn't problem solving, it's something that soothes, that comforts, just being there."

Once I started reading about emotional eating and realized that's what was going on with me, I explained it to my mom and said that her ways of dealing with food and her body wouldn't work for someone like me. I explained to her that dieting would

---

Being completely honest and frank about your food and weight issues with your loved ones, asking for exactly what you need, and telling them exactly what you don't, is incredibly important. Not just for your recovery, but for your relationship.

---

not cure me, and also told her flat out that I needed her to re-
frain from giving me advice (even if, at a weak moment, I asked
for it!). I was finding my own path of recovery, and as hard as it
might be for her to watch me struggle through it, that's exactly
what I needed her to do. Being straight with my mom saved
both of us a lot of pain, too. She no longer had to feel responsible for fixing me; I no longer had to resent her for giving me the
"wrong" kind of help.

Not everyone's parents or loved ones are going to understand. In cases like that, Dr. Lukens said you pretty much have
to put your foot down and tell them to mind their own business.
"When I go home, and we go out to eat at a restaurant and I
order a slice of cake for dessert, there's my mom—in *public*—telling me, 'Stop it! That's enough!' when I've taken two bites," Trish
told me. "I get embarrassed and feel ashamed. It was one thing
for her to do this to me growing up, but now I'm a fully capable
adult and she still thinks she has to tell me when to stop eating,
like I'm some barnyard animal. When I went home for Thanksgiving, and my dad mentioned something about a pecan pie, my
mom looked at me and said, 'Oh no, you can't have that,' and I
finally told her to leave me alone. I said I didn't want her to even
look toward my plate at Thanksgiving dinner. I told her I didn't
want to hear her say one word about what I was eating, because
I wanted to enjoy my weekend and that it needs to stop. I'm an
adult now, not a child."

I believe that being completely honest and frank about your food and weight issues with your loved ones, asking for exactly what you need and telling them exactly what you don't, is incredibly important. Not just for your recovery, but for your relationship. Jenelle told me that explaining to her mom just how bad things were has been helpful. "I tend to sugarcoat my problems so as to not upset anyone around me, but this past weekend I really opened up to my mother," she said. "Though the word is scary, it helped to describe my problems with the word *disorder* and explain to her that I lost weight not through dieting but through 'starvation' and 'deprivation.' She opened up to me about her own body issues and my father's food issues. I opened up to her about my food sneaking and overeating that she didn't know about throughout childhood and high school. She fully supports me and wants me to get help. Knowing that I can call her and talk through my emotions when I feel a binge coming on comforts me."

For many years, my mother and I rarely, if ever, talked about food or our bodies. But eventually, as I healed and became stronger in my recovery, we began to share about that stuff again. She told me a couple of years ago that, through our discussions, she's come to understand that she's a bit weird about food, too—and she thanked me for helping her figure it out. Amazing, right? Recovery doesn't just help us with our food and weight issues, it helps heal our relationships, too.

Your Turn:

1. Have you been open with close friends about your food issues? If so, has it helped? If not, do you think it would help you to let go of some shame if you opened up to a trusted friend or two?

2. Do you have any friends whose body bashing or food issues trigger negative feelings in you? What can you do or say to protect yourself from this in the future?

3. How have food or weight issues affected your social life?

4. If you live with a significant other, are there things you can ask your partner to do (or not do) that will help your recovery? Are you willing to have that discussion?

5. Did your parents ever—or do they now—say hurtful things to you about food or your body? Do you think that they want to help, but don't know how?

6. If someone making painful food and body comments is an ongoing issue in your life, what can you do or say to establish your boundaries and express to these people what it is you need from them?

chapter ten

What Life Is Like When You Get Sane About Food

You've come to the end of this book, but your journey of healing your relationship with food may be just beginning. Recovering from binge eating has been a long haul for me, but I don't regret one moment of the last fifteen years. Every binge, every weigh-in, every diet, every book I read, every fat day, every journal page filled with teary truths about my life and my body, is what it took to get to where I am now: healthy, happy, and pretty darn sane about food.

It's no mystery how I got here. If you look back over the chapters, it's easy to see a clear, step-by-step path. I got discouraged along the way, tired of fighting, but I never gave up, and neither can you. No matter how hard things get, you must keep moving slowly, steadily, gently forward. That's how you'll get to freedom and recovery—and when you do, you're going to be blown away by how good it feels.

What Does Being "Recovered" Really Mean?

As I've admitted in these pages, on rare occasions I may give in to an emotional urge to eat. Still, I describe myself as being recovered. I say that because, by definition, someone with BED binges frequently, feels disgusted and shamed after overeating, feels a loss of control, and, perhaps most important, the eating behaviors negatively affect other aspects of their lives.

None of those things is true for me anymore and hasn't been for a very long time. Does "recovered" mean I never, ever eat something for a reason other than hunger or accidentally overdo it at dinner? No. But you know what? Totally normal eaters do those things once in a while, too. Being a normal and sane eater doesn't mean being a *perfect* eater.

"Recovery looks different for everyone," nutrition therapist Juliet Zuercher, R.D., told me. "It's possible to have some disordered traits, but at the same time live your life in fullness and freedom. I think maybe one out of a thousand has a kind of conversion experience where they just turn their back on their disorder and really don't have eating issues again. It's much more likely that these thoughts will bounce up sometimes in your life."

Erica's overeating hasn't completely disappeared, but she's noticed big differences in the severity of her binges and feels much less helpless now than she did even a year ago. "Now that I'm recovering, my binges are much smaller and are much less frequent," she told me. "I would say they happen on average about two to three times a month now, depending on what I'm going through, instead of several times a week. I differentiate a binge from a slight overindulgence not necessarily by how much I eat anymore—it's more about why I'm overeating. I'll ask myself, 'Was what I ate really so amazing that I just wanted more, or was I using it as a coping mechanism?' If it's the latter, I consider it a binge."

It's important as you go forward to take the time to notice

We can't control whether our thoughts turn to food when a difficult emotion pops up, but in recovery we have some control over what we *do* with those thoughts. To binge or not to binge becomes a choice.

---

all the little ways your relationship with food is changing. "Another difference is that at the height of my bingeing, I didn't feel like I could control myself," said Erica. "If I felt the urge to binge, some zombielike state would come over me and I could not get the food out of my mind until I consumed it. Now when I binge, I feel that it's almost out of laziness; I'll have cravings that I know in my head I probably could fight, but I give in to them anyway. Part of me is so used to having given in for so long that occasionally I still do instead of using tactics that I learned in therapy."

We can't control whether or not our thoughts turn to food when a difficult emotion pops up, but like Erica mentioned, in recovery we have some control over what we *do* with those thoughts. To binge or not to binge becomes a choice. We have other coping strategies and tools in our toolboxes now—and the more we choose to use them instead of turning to food, the easier it is to do the same the next time, and the time after that.

"Getting better from binge eating disorder isn't like turning a switch on and off," Shannon told me. "Recovery is a process, but I have the tools now to engage in that fight through increased self-awareness. Most days remain difficult, but I continue to write and journal and really pay attention to why I want to eat."

Why It's Important to Celebrate
All Your Little Victories

Many emotional overeaters tend to downplay positive things in life, especially about themselves. That's one reason why acknowledging every tiny step forward in this journey is important. "Truly acknowledging the little victories helped me put in perspective the small changes I was making—soon I had a whole basket full of little victories, which equaled bigger ones and eventually great progress," Morgan told me. One of her little victories? "I was having a bit of an off week and was at my parents' house for the holidays," she said. "I was home alone and I opened the familiar cabinet that holds the cereal, and I just stared at it and thought: 'That doesn't even seem appealing one bit. Dry cereal? No way.' I closed the cabinet and made myself some tea. It was kind of amazing that I truly didn't even want it even though I had been having some challenging times."

Little victories don't have to be about food. They can be about getting to know yourself better, like for Kate, who recently recognized that a difficult talk with a coworker had put her in danger of bingeing. "I managed to drive to the gym after work that day, but sat in my car for ten minutes trying to decide if I wanted to go to yoga, or if I wanted to go home," she said. "I realized that I really need to go to yoga at that moment because if I went straight home I was setting myself up for a binge. An hour later, after the class, I felt better about the situation and ready to face the new work challenges I have coming up." For Jenn, a recent little victory was being able to stop herself when she realized she was munching out of boredom. "I was eating small handfuls of homemade granola—really just mindlessly snacking—and then I thought, 'Why am I eating this? Am I really hungry?'" she said. "It made me put the handful back and put the lid back on and walk away. And I didn't obsess about going back for more. I've been trying to increase my self-awareness about why I'm eating things and refraining if I'm not hungry, so this was a big victory for me."

Letting Go of the Good Girl's Drug Is Hard, but It's So Worth It

From the little things ("It's beautiful to be able to have a donut and not feel guilty about it!" said Erica) to the major game changers, life is infinitely more lovely when you're not abusing food. I mean, it's still life—there's plenty of pain and difficulty—but when you feel hope and are actively engaged in living, even the tough stuff has beauty to it.

Erica told me that even though she is having a hard time in

her life, she is proud and amazed by the way she is handling it. "I'm going through the aftermath of a horrible breakup, but the healthy eating and exercising habits that I've formed over the past few years have not been shaken," she said. "The anger and disappointment I'm feeling makes me want to get up in the morning and let off some steam at the gym. The sadness and sluggishness I feel makes me want to eat healthy foods that will give me more energy to get through the day. To be honest, my life is the toughest it's ever been right now. If I had been faced with all this a few years ago, I would've crumbled. But here I am, still standing—and it feels good."

When your mind isn't drugged by food and you feel clear-headed and competent, it's amazing what can happen. "Being fearless when it comes to food has made me less fearful in general," Casey told me. "There was a time when I would avoid going to dinner parties or grabbing drinks with friends because I was so concerned about consuming empty calories, and even more concerned with finding myself in a situation that might spark a binge. Sometimes I still get stressed out and want to grab a package of Mint Milanos and devour them faster than you can say 'Pepperidge Farm.' But eating well, being patient with myself, and relieving stress in ways that don't involve over-eating like yoga, running, and writing have changed the way I live."

Anna is reveling in the changes she's experienced, too.

"There is this magic in realizing that you deserve love and healing rather than punitive judgment. It frees you to take real, good, wholehearted care of yourself," she said. "I feel victorious when I brush my teeth before bed, or when I feed myself healthy food. I am so filled with gratitude every time I dance on a crowded dance floor, not worried about who's watching me, or what my body looks like. When I talk to people about how I'm feeling rather than stuffing it all down under giant amounts of buttered popcorn, I'm actually growing and living. Basically, feeling good more than I feel bad is a thrilling new fact of my life and I am so grateful I've had the opportunity to heal, no matter how hard the struggle can be at times."

It takes patience and a lot of courage to fix your relationship with food—if you dig deep enough, you'll find that you have plenty of both. "The payoff is real and recovery has been accomplished by millions," said Dr. Lukens. "That being said, you're going to have to work at it and you might not see the light at the end of the tunnel for a long time. I sometimes describe it as standing on one side of a rickety-looking old bridge. It's really long and you almost need binoculars to see that there is some-

---

Being fearless when it comes to food will make us less fearful in general.

---

thing on the other side. You might feel at some point like the wind has kicked up and the bridge is swaying back and forth. You're gonna be even more scared than you are now. It might feel like it gets worse before it gets better."

But it does get better.

I no longer fight or struggle daily with food. Cravings, weight concerns, and food thoughts no longer have power over my life or cloud my brain. I feel free.

When my bingeing was at its worst, I didn't believe this kind of change was possible for me. I couldn't even see that rickety old "recovery bridge" that Dr. Lukens talked about, let alone picture myself stepping out onto it. But now, standing on the other side, I just want to call out to every single one of you, "Come across, it's freakin' awesome over here!"

Don't wait—just run for it.

Your Turn:

1. Do you believe recovery is possible? How does hearing how things have changed for me, Morgan, Casey, Anna, and Erica make you feel about the future of your own relationship with food?

2. What little victories have you had in your journey lately?

3. How can you make acknowledging these small steps forward a part of your daily life (write about one victory each

morning, for example, or take a weekly "victory lap" in which you give yourself five minutes to reflect on at least one positive thing that happened)?

4. Now, what is the next step you are going to take in your recovery? Turn the page if you need some ideas.

Where to Go for More Help

Support Groups 101:
How to Find One Near You

"I went to a support group in the town that my college was located in—I found the group by just searching online," said Morgan. "It was offered through an adult education system that the city had. At first it can seem scary and intimidating, but taking that first step and showing up makes all the difference, and it feels really good to have a source of support." You can start by simply Googling "eating disorder support groups" or "binge eating support groups" in your area like Morgan did—or you can start with these organizations and websites to find groups near you:

National Eating Disorders Association

NEDA has a help line that's open to calls Monday through Friday from 8:30 to 4:30, Pacific standard time, where you can get information, therapist referrals, and help tracking down support meetings: 800-931-2237, www.nationaleatingdisorders.org.

Binge Eating Disorder Association

Although BEDA doesn't host its own support groups, the site has a growing list of groups and meetings and a listing of other support sites: www.bedaonline.org.

Eating Disorders Anonymous

This twelve-step group has meetings in thirty-two states, plus all-volunteer hotlines and phone meetings that you can call in to no matter where you live: www.eatingdisordersanonymous.org.

Overeaters Anonymous

Another twelve-step group, but this one has meetings and chapters in all fifty states and internationally, as well as phone and online meetings if there isn't a group in your town or you don't feel ready for a face-to-face meeting: www.oa.org.

EDReferral.com

This site has a huge listing of free meetings in thirty-five states and Canada, plus referrals to therapists.

Campus Psychological or Health Services
Part-time and full-time college students often have free—or superdiscounted—access to group meetings or therapy sessions.

Further Reading:
Recommended Books

These are all books that I've read myself or that were suggested by experts I interviewed for this book.

Feeding the Hungry Heart by Geneen Roth

The Body Image Workbook by Thomas Cash, Ph.D.

Intuitive Eating: A Revolutionary Program That Works by Evelyn Tribole, M.S., R.D., and Elyse Resch, M.S., R.D.

Crave: Why You Binge Eat and How to Stop by Cynthia Bulik, M.D.

Overcoming Binge Eating by Christopher Fairburn, M.D.

The End of Overeating by David Kessler, M.D.

Eating in the Light of the Moon by Anita Johnston, Ph.D.

Breaking Free from Emotional Eating by Geneen Roth

Life Beyond Your Eating Disorder by Johanna Kandel, founder of the Alliance for Eating Disorders Awareness

Online Resources: Recommended Websites

HealthyGirl.org

My online support site for girls and young women who binge or emotionally overeat.

SomethingFishy.org

A well-established site for information about all types of eating disorders, plus moderated forums, therapist referrals, and other information.

NationalEatingDisorders.org

The website of the National Eating Disorders Association.

BEDAonline.org

The website of the Binge Eating Disorder Association.

AllianceForEatingDisorders.org

The website of the Alliance for Eating Disorders Awareness, which offers information on body image, eating disorders of all kinds, and help finding support groups, therapy, and other treatment options in your area.

BodyImageProject.com

A site that shares videos and readings about improving body image, co-founded by Tiffany Stewart, Ph.D.

Eating Disorder Treatment Centers: Inpatient and Outpatient Programs

Many eating disorder treatment centers offer inpatient and outpatient care not just for anorexia and bulimia, but for binge eating and emotional eating, too. This is a short list of excellent centers where some of my favorite therapists and experts work—but there are many more facilities all around the country. Check nationaleatingdisorders.org for a more complete listing or talk to your doctor or therapist for a referral.

The Renfrew Center

Programs for anorexia, bulimia, and binge eating disorder; locations in Pennsylvania, Florida, New Jersey, New York, Connecticut, North Carolina, Tennessee, Texas, and Maryland. www .renfrewcenter.com

Remuda Ranch

Programs for anorexia, bulimia, emotional eating, and anxiety; locations in Arizona and Virginia. www.remudaranch.com

University of North Carolina Eating Disorders Program

Programs for a range of eating disorders; located in Chapel Hill, North Carolina. www.psychiatry.unc.edu/eatingdisorders

Eating Recovery Center

Programs for a range of eating disorders; location in Denver, Colorado. www.Eatingrecoverycenter.com

Monte Nido Treatment Centers

Programs for anorexia, bulimia, and exercise addiction; locations in Malibu and Brentwood, California, and Eugene, Oregon. www.montenido.com

sources cited

American Psychiatric Association. *DSM-V Proposed Diagnostic Criteria for Binge Eating Disorder* (October 6, 2010), http://www.dsm5.org/ProposedRevisions/Pages/proposedrevision.aspx?rid=372, accessed on November 26, 2010.

American Psychological Association. *Stress in America 2010 report* (2010).

Araujo, D. M. "Binge eating disorder and depression: a systematic review," *World Journal of Biological Psychiatry,* 11(2 Pt 2) (March 2010), 199–207.

Azarbad, L. "Psychosocial correlates of binge eating in Hispanic, African American, and Caucasian women presenting for bariatric surgery," *Eating Behaviors,* 11(2), (April 2010) 79–84.

Binge Eating Disorder Association. *Binge Eating Disorder,* http://www.bedaonline.com/abouted/BED.html, accessed November 26, 2010.

Bulik, C. M. "The relation between eating disorders and components of perfectionism," *American Journal of Psychiatry,* 160(2) (February 2003), 366–368.

———. *Why You Binge Eat and How to Stop* (New York: Walker Publishing Company, Inc., 2009).

Cash, T. F. *The BodyImage Workbook: An Eight-Step Program for Learning to Like Your Looks* (Oakland, CA: New Harbinger Publications, Inc., 2008).

Cottone, P. "Consummatory, anxiety-related and metabolic adaptations in female rats with alternating access to preferred food," *Psychoneuroendocrinology,* 34(1) (January 2009), 38–49.

Cottone, P. "Opioid-dependent anticipatory negative contrast and binge-like eating in rats with limited access to highly preferred food." *Neuropsychopharmacology,* 33(3) (February 2008), 524–535.

Davidson, R. J. " Alterations in brain and immune function produced my mindfulness meditation," *Psychosomatic Medicine,* 65(4) (2003), 564–570.

Dotinga, R. "Study links yo-yo dieting to addiction," HealthDay news/*US News and World Report* online (November 12, 2009), http://health.usnews.com/health-news/family-health/brain-and-behavior/articles/2009/11/12/study-links-yo-yo-dieting-to-addiction.html, accessed November 27, 2010.

Grumman, R. "Why we eat too much and how to get control," *Health* (September 18, 2009), http://www.cnn.com/2009/HEALTH/09/18/why.overeat.eat .much/index.html, accessed November 27, 2010.

Heller, T. *Eating Disorders: A Handbook forTeens, Families and Teachers* (Jefferson, N.C.: McFarland & Company, Inc., 2003).

Hudson, J. I. "The prevalence and correlates of eating disorders in the National Comorbidity Survey Replication." *Biological Psychiatry,* 61(3) (2007), 348–358.

Hudson, J. I. "Binge-eating disorder as a distinct familial phenotype in obese individuals," *Archives of General Psychiatry,* 63(3) (March 2006), 313–319.

Javaras, K. N. "Familiality and heritability of binge eating disorder: results of a case-control family study and a twin study," *International Journal of Eating Disorders,* 41(2) (March 2008), 174–179.

Johnston, A. *Eating in the Light of the Moon: How Women Can Transform Their Relationship with Food Through Myths, Metaphors, and Storytelling* (Carlsbad: Gürze Books, 2000).

Kristeller, J. L. "An exploratory study of a meditation-based intervention for binge eating disorder." *Journal of Health Psychology,* 4(3) (July 1999), 357–363.

Meno, C. A. "Familial and individual variables as predictors of dieting concerns and binge eating in college females," *Eating Behaviors* 9(1) (January 2008), 91–101.

Monteleone, P. "Genetic susceptibility to eating disorders: associated polymorphisms and pharmacogenetic suggestions," *Pharmacogenomics*, 9(10), (October 2008) 1487–1520.

Neumark-Sztainer. *"I'm, Like, SO Fat!": Helping Your Teen Make Healthy Choices about Eating and Exercise in a Weight-Obsessed World* (New York: The Guilford Press, 2005).

Radcliffe, R. *Enlightened Eating: Understanding and Changing YourRelationship with Food* (Minneapolis: Ease, 1996).

Roth, G. *Women, Food and God: An Unexpected Path to Almost Everything* (New York: Scribner, 2010).

Sonder, B. *Eating Disorders: When Food Turns Against You* (London: Franklin Watts, 1993).

Stang J., Story M. *Guidelines for Adolescent Nutrition Services, 2005.* http://www.epi.umn.edu/let/pubs/adol_book.shtm, accessed November 27, 2010.

Tanofsky-Kraff, M. "Loss of control eating disorder in children age 12 years and younger: proposed research criteria," *Eating Behaviors*, 9(3) (2008), 360–365.

The National Institute of Mental Health. *Eating Disorders: Facts About Eating Disorders and the Search for Solutions* (2001).

Tobin, D. "Early trauma, dissociation, and late onset in the eating disorders," *International Journal of Eating Disorders*, 17(3) (April 1995), 305–308.

Wonderlich, S. A. (2001, December). "Eating disturbance and sexual trauma in childhood and adulthood," *International Journal of Eating Disorders*, 30(4), (December 2001), 401–412.

experts

Cynthia M. Bulik, Ph.D.

Dr. Bulik is the William R. and Jeanne H. Jordan Distinguished Professor of Eating Disorders in the psychiatry department of the School of Medicine at the University of North Carolina at Chapel Hill. She is also a professor of nutrition in the Gillings School of Global Public Health and the Director of the University of North Carolina Eating Disorders Program. She has written more than 380 scientific papers and chapters on eating disorders and her research collaborations have been key in establishing the hereditary nature of eating disorders. Dr. Bulik is the author of several books including *Crave: Why You Binge Eat and How to Stop* (Walker & Company, 2009) and *Runaway Eating: The 8-Point Plan to Conquer Adult Food and Weight Obsessions* (Rodale, 2005). You can find her online at unceatingdisorders.org and twitter.com/cbulik.

Liza Feilner, M.A.

Feilner is an eating disorders therapist and body image specialist at the Remuda Ranch eating disorder treatment center in Wickenburg, Arizona.

Amy Jaffe, M.S., R.D., L.D.

Jaffe is a nutrition therapist in private practice at Miami Counseling and Resource Center in Miami, Florida, where she specializes in weight management issues and in the treatment of children, women, and men with eating disorders, including anorexia, bulimia, and compulsive overeating. She also consults at an intensive outpatient program for eating disorders in Hollywood, Florida. Jaffe was a professor of dietetics and nutrition at Florida International University for eighteen years and has also worked at Miami Children's Hospital and the Renfrew Center eating disorders clinic in Coral Gables, Florida.

Kathy Kaehler

Kaehler is a Los Angeles fitness trainer who's worked with stars like Jennifer Aniston, Denise Richards, Julia Roberts, and Kim Kardashian. A former bulimic, Kaehler is now an ambassador for the Alliance for Eating Disorders Awareness. She's the author of several fitness books, including *Teenage Fitness* and *Kathy Kaehler's Sunday Set-Up*. Her website is www.kathykaehler.net.

Michael D. Lukens, Ph.D.

Dr. Lukens is a psychologist and clinical director of SeaSide Palm Beach, an executive drug and alcohol rehabilitation program in Palm Beach, Florida. He has been working one on one with addicts and emotional eaters for more than twenty-two years and offers seminars and small group workshops on emotional eating on the web and in-person in South Florida. His website: stopemotionaleating.org.

Andrea Mitchell

Mitchell is a licensed art psychotherapist, certified Reiki practitioner, and mind-body fitness expert in New York City. She has worked as a fitness trainer with actors like Anna Paquin, Julia Stiles, and Piper Perabo. Her website is themitchellmethod.com.

Jennifer Nardozzi, Psy.D.

Dr. Nardozzi is a psychologist who specializes in treating women with eating disorders. She has a private practice in Coral Gables, Florida, and is the national training manager of the Renfrew Center eating disorders clinic. She has led dozens of workshops and trainings on the mind-body-spirit connection and other topics at national conferences and seminars around the United States and in Russia and Uganda.

Drew Pinsky, M.D.

Dr. Pinsky is an addiction medicine specialist, host of *Celebrity Rehab with Dr. Drew*, co-host of the long-running radio show *Loveline*, and author of the *New York Times* bestselling book *The Mirror Effect: How Celebrity Narcissism Is Seducing America*. His website is DrDrew.com.

Rebecca Radcliffe

Radcliffe is an expert on body image, eating, and women's issues and the author of several books including *Enlightened Eating: Understanding & Changing Your Relationship with Food* and *Finding Body Peace: A Journey of Self-Acceptance*. You can find her online at rebeccaradcliffe.com.

Charles Sophy, F.A.C.N.

Dr. Sophy is a psychiatrist in private practice and serves as the medical director for the Los Angeles County Department of Children and Family Services, the nation's largest foster care operation. He is also a clinical instructor at the University of California, Los Angeles Neuro-Psychiatric Institute. Dr. Sophy is the author of *Side By Side: The Revolutionary Mother-Daughter Program for Conflict-Free Communication* and has been interviewed as a mental health expert by press outlets ranging from the *Washington Post* to the *Today Show*. His website is drsophy.com.

Tiffany Stewart, Ph.D.

Dr. Stewart is a researcher at the Pennington Biomedical Research Center in Baton Rouge, Louisiana, where she focuses on the assessment, prevention, and treatment of body image disturbance, eating disorders, and obesity. Her work also includes the development of technologically advanced assessment measures for eating disorders, including computerized body image technology. She is the co-founder and chief scientific officer of Body Evolution Technologies, Inc., an early stage digital media company that develops body image assessment and intervention programs. Her websites include bodyimage project.com and Emer.ge.

Marian Tanofsky-Kraff, Ph.D.

Dr. Tanofsky-Kraff is an associate professor of medical and clinical psychology at the Uniformed Services University of the Health Sciences and a researcher at the Eunice Kennedy Shriver National Institute of Child Health and Human Development (part of the National Institutes of Health) in Bethesda, Maryland. She studies eating disorders, binge eating, and obesity in children and adolescents, is the author of dozens of clinical studies on the topic, and is testing a psychotherapeutic program to prevent excessive weight in girls at high risk for obesity.

Juliet Zuercher, R.D.

Zuercher is a registered dietitian who works with emotional eaters and disordered eaters at Timberline Knolls Residential Treatment Center, My Balanced Life Integrative Counseling center, and Doorways Counseling and Psychiatric Services for Adolescents and Young Adults in Phoenix, Arizona. She uses the Health at Every Size approach to help her clients restore a healthy relationship with food, and spent twelve years as a dietitian at Remuda Ranch.

notes

notes

notes

notes